JIM FOWLER'S
WILDEST
PLACES
ON EARTH

JIM FOWLER'S
WILDEST
PLACES
ON EARTH

PRESENTED BY  AND

MUTUAL OF OMAHA'S
WILDLIFE HERITAGE TRUST

TIME
LIFE
CUSTOM
PUBLISHING

Jim Fowler's WILDEST PLACES ON EARTH was produced for Time-Life Custom Publishing and Mutual of Omaha by

ST. REMY PRESS

PUBLISHER	Kenneth Winchester
PRESIDENT	Pierre Léveillé
Senior Editor	Brian Parsons
Art Director	Philippe Arnoldi
Contributing Editor	David Dunbar
Picture Editor	Christopher Jackson
Contributing Researchers	Olga Dzatko, Sandra Snow
Designers	Hélène Dion, Sara Grynspan
Proofreader	Judy Yelon
Managing Editor	Carolyn Jackson
Managing Art Director	Diane Denoncourt
Administrator	Natalie Watanabe
Production Manager	Michelle Turbide
System Coordinator	Jean-Luc Roy

Time-Life Books is a division of
TIME LIFE INCORPORATED

President and CEO	John M. Fahey, Jr.
President, Time-Life Books	John D. Hall

TIME-LIFE CUSTOM PUBLISHING

Vice President and Publisher	Susan J. Maruyama
Editorial Director	Robert A. Doyle
Operations Manager	Phyllis A. Gardner
Production Manager	Prudence G. Harris
Promotions Managers	Becky Wheeler, Gary Stoiber
Retail Director	Christine S. Benjamin
Retail Sales Manager	Lorna Milkovich
Sales Director	Frances C. Mangan
Special Contributors	Dana Coleman, Patricia Loushine, Becky Merson, Tracey Warner

MUTUAL OF OMAHA COMPANIES

Vice President and Director of Public Affairs	Terry A. Calek

BOZELL WORLDWIDE

Senior Vice President	Phillip G. Webb

THE WRITERS

Douglas H. Chadwick is a field biologist, conservationist and freelance writer whose most recent book is *The Fate of the Elephant.* His assignments for *National Geographic* and other publications have taken him to wild lands throughout the world for more than two decades.

George Harrison is a nature writer, photographer, book author and consultant who has traveled to 50 countries on five continents in pursuit of outdoor adventures. He is field editor of *National/International Wildlife*, nature editor of *Sports Afield* and president of Harrison Productions, Inc., a nature communications firm in Hubertus, Wisconsin.

Kim Heacox, a former park ranger and biologist, has authored and photographed two books on Alaska: *Iditarod Spirit* and *In Denali.* In 1987 and 1990 he won the Lowell Thomas Award for excellence in travel journalism.

Bern Keating has worked in 110 countries during his 50-year career as a freelance journalist for publications such as *National Geographic, Travel & Leisure,* and *Smithsonian.* In recent decades he has concentrated on wildlife conservation, especially in Africa and India.

Les Line was editor-in-chief of *Audubon,* magazine of the National Audubon Society, for 25 years. He is the author, photographer, or editor of some 30 books on natural history and wildlife conservation.

Pat and **Baiba Morrow** have shared assignments on all seven continents. They have documented their climbing, skiing and cultural travel experiences in magazines, newspapers, books, multi-media presentations, and more recently, on film and video. They live in Canmore, Alberta.

Boyd Norton has been a photographer and writer for more than 20 years, specializing in global issues of wilderness, wildlife and the environment. He is the author-photographer of more than 12 books and his work has been featured in major magazines worldwide.

Greg Stott is a Toronto-based writer, photographer and film/video producer. He has traveled to more than 55 countries, and has contributed to several books and leading publications. His latest long-term project is introducing his three-year-old son, Jeremy, to the wonders and challenges of the planet earth.

Fowler, Jim, 1930-
(Wildest places on earth)
Jim Fowler's wildest places on earth.
   p. cm.
Includes bibliographical references.
ISBN 0-8094-6688-0 $39.95
1. Natural history. 2. Natural history—Pictorial works.
I. Title. II. title: Wildest places on earth.
QH45.5.F68   1993
508–dc20   93-1139
               CIP

For information about any Time-Life book, please call 1-800-621-7026, or write:
Reader Information
Time-Life Customer Service
P.O. Box C-32068
Richmond, Virginia
23261-2068

Cliffs of sandstone, a sedimentary rock that makes up less than five percent of the earth's crust, glint beneath the clouds over Australia's Rainbow Valley National Park.

Survivors of a once-abundant species, bison graze a lush meadow in North America's Yellowstone National Park—a vast, volcanic plateau and mountain region.

Member of a marine plunge-diver family that has flown the earth for at least 20 million years, a lone red-footed booby rests a moment in South America's Galápagos Islands.

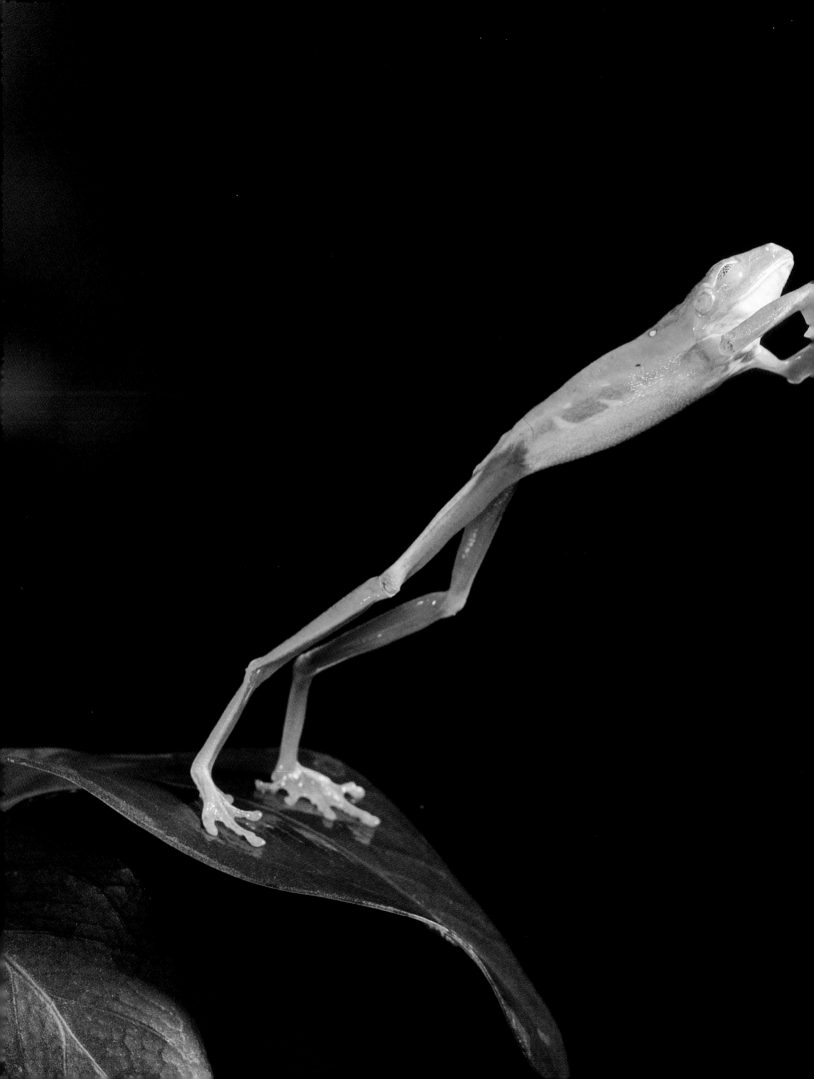

Leaping by night through a soggy rain forest in Central America, a red-eyed leaf frog makes use of its toe disks and sticky foot webbing to grip slippery foliage.

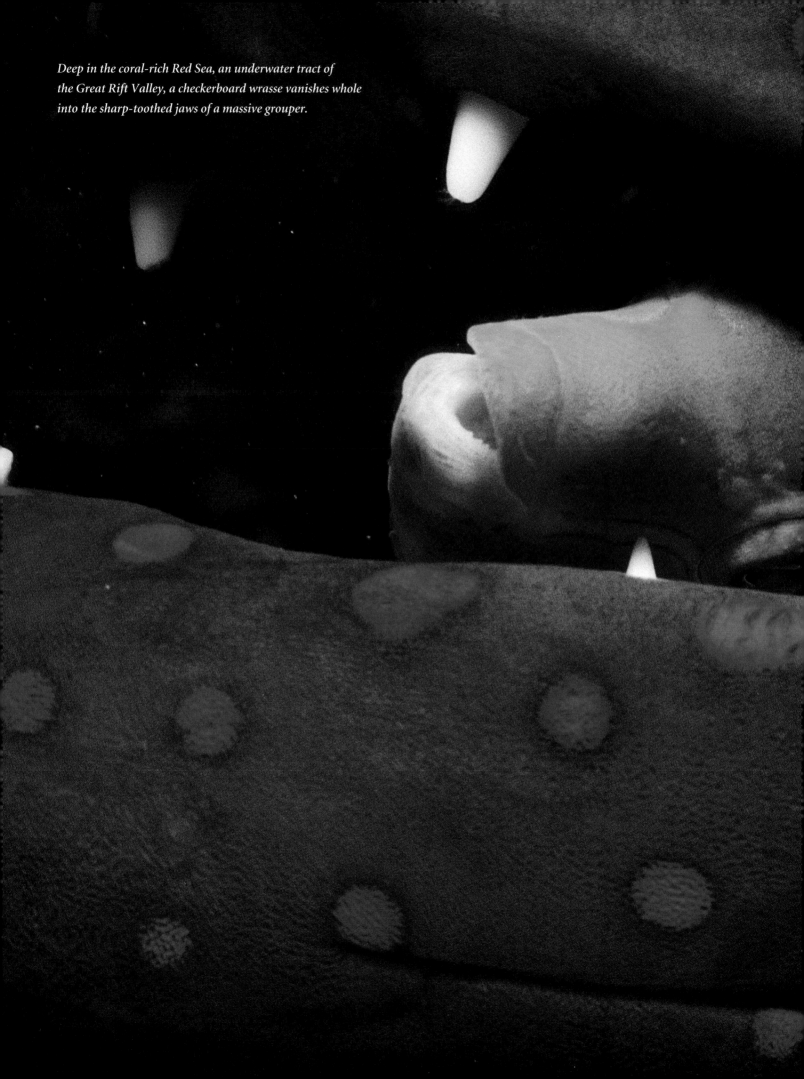

Deep in the coral-rich Red Sea, an underwater tract of
the Great Rift Valley, a checkerboard wrasse vanishes whole
into the sharp-toothed jaws of a massive grouper.

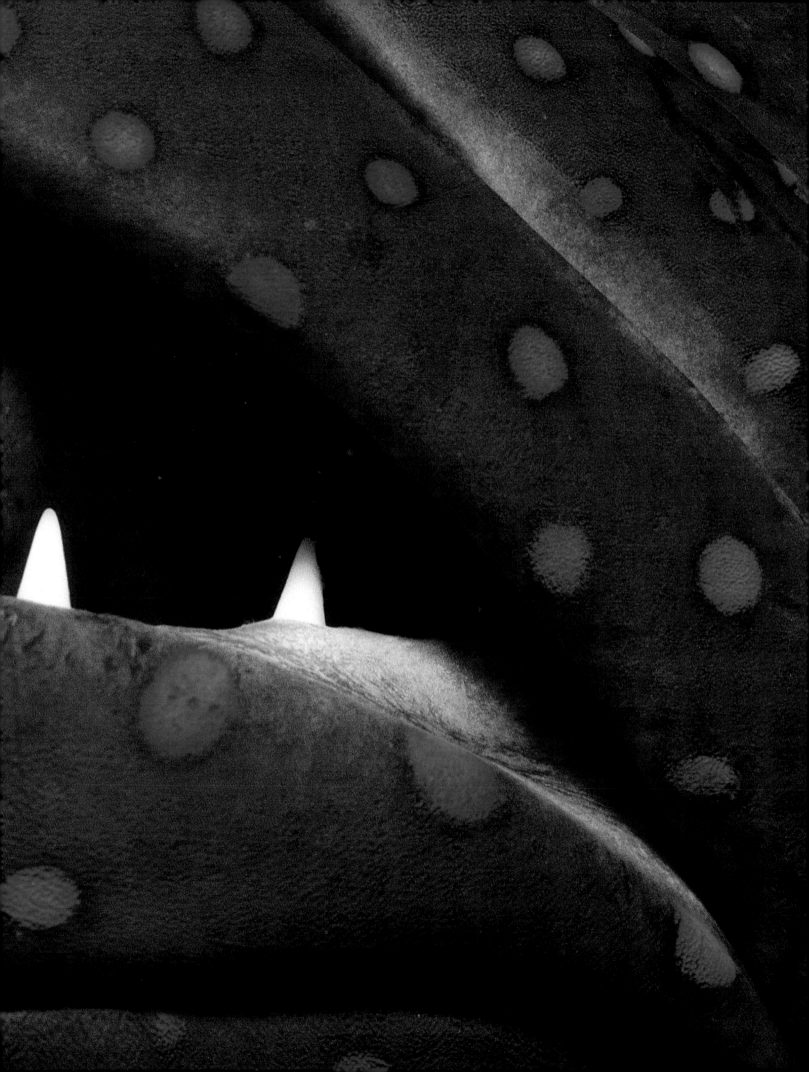

Isolated from other land some 100 million years ago, Australia became home to the great gray kangaroo, a fast-moving marsupial with a unique, jumping method of locomotion.

A red lechwe sprints through Africa's Okavango Delta, an unusual alluvial conduit that each year dumps billions of cubic feet of fresh water into the Kalahari Desert.

CONTENTS

BROOKS RANGE

The GeoSphere Image was created from thousands of individual high-resolution satellite images that were assembled electronically.

RORAIMA

OKAVANGO DELTA

SKELETON COAST

TORRES DEL PAINE

ANTARCTIC
PENINSULA

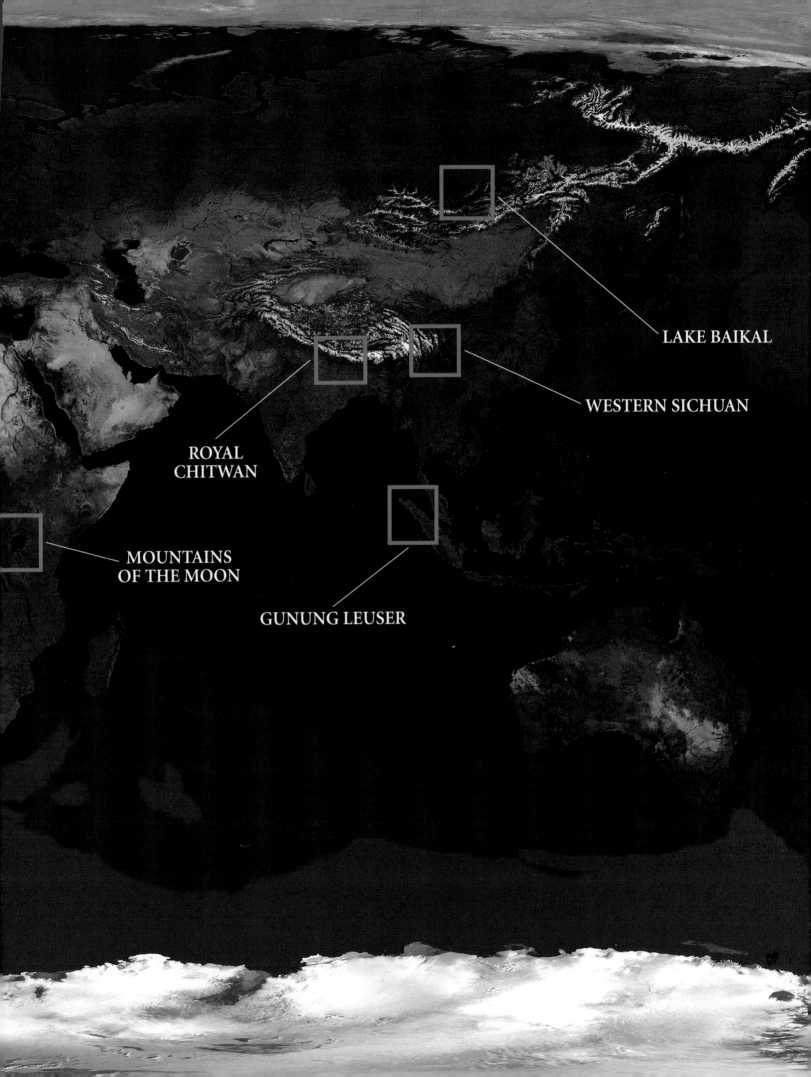

LAKE BAIKAL

WESTERN SICHUAN

ROYAL
CHITWAN

MOUNTAINS
OF THE MOON

GUNUNG LEUSER

FOREWORD

*I*N 1969 RADIO BROADCASTER LOWELL THOMAS, Honory President of the Explorer's Club, told me that one fifth of the earth's land surface was still largely unexplored. Skeptical, I thought for a moment and realized that he was probably right. Twenty-four years and many frequent-flyer miles later, I found myself giving similar assurance to a flight attendant who had asked me if there were any truly wild places left in the world for her to visit with her eight-year-old daughter.

There must be something that people are born with or learn from others—maybe a combination of both—that makes them "turn on" to nature and seek adventure. In my case, I remember well the anticipation that I felt as a boy when my dad loaded my brothers and me into the car for the 12-mile trip to our farm at Mud Creek in Georgia.

We once stopped abruptly on the road to the house to let an alligator cross; it was the first one I had ever seen. In the eyes of a six-year-old, which I was at the time, the alligator was at least 20 feet long, easily as large as our 1936 Buick sedan. I now realize that this would have been a record, since 15 feet is about as long as alligators get. In its hurry to flee, this big old guy tried again and again to launch itself over an embankment back into the safety of the swamp. I have never forgotten my excitement, amazement and sense of awe. The scene of the alligator flipping over, spinning around and trying to run away is etched in my mind forever.

Other adventures in what seemed a vast, unexplored wilderness along Mud Creek—catching snakes, collecting exoskeletons of cicadas off the bark of pine trees, watching a forest fire race through the woods—fed my dream of someday exploring far-off wild places. Lying on the front porch at night in the summer heat, I wondered what there was in the darkness around me. Since I did not consider wilderness to be a hostile environment, I never thought of animals as creatures of the night that would do me harm. Only much later, after I had seen a few Tarzan movies, did I begin to imagine gorillas coming up onto the porch. Then I started shutting the screen door behind me.

After I had majored in zoology at Earlham College in Richmond, Indiana, I went to Florida to train eagles, a pursuit that in 1957 took me to Africa—my first trip to a distant wild place. While traveling with a clan of nomadic bushmen who lived north of the Okavango Delta in what was then Bechuanaland, I began to understand the true meaning of wildness. The bushmen wandered through their world oblivious to the one from which I had come. Their family life was natural, genuine and caring, based on fundamental biological laws of harmony and survival. The children were happy and played with homemade toys. When I pointed to Sputnik, the first satellite, and tried to explain it, the bushmen just asked, "Why?"

At night I sensed the connectedness of the bushmen, their small fires and their closeness with the reflected moonlight, the stars blinking in the endless sky and whatever there was that lay further beyond. Everything around me, I realized, was a product of natural forces. The sun, the wind, the rain, the seasons and the position of the planet were responsible for the trees, the sand, the animals, the waterholes and the bushmen. Nothing had been formed by humans. Only I was out of place, an outsider observing from a distance.

I was already comfortable with nature. From the bushmen, however, I learned to be comfortable with wildness. Requirements for survival were fairly simple. Food was readily available if one knew where to get it. Insects were not that bad. Sleeping on a grass mat kept away the night chill. Wildness may have to do with physical proper-

Jim Fowler at the Explorer's
Club in New York City.

ties, but I discovered that comfort is mostly a sense of
well-being and a knowledge of the surroundings.

For me, the thrill of wildness used to lie in its mystery.
Now, I am equally enthralled by the complexities of wildness and by the ways in which humans are an intricate
piece of the puzzle. By helping to record its diversity and
document efforts to preserve its many forms, my goal has
been to present information on wildness that stimulates
interest and encourages respect. Millions of people around
the world have discovered the excitement of adventure in
the wilderness. Now, attention to the world's wilderness
centers on the question of whether or not it can be saved.

We are indisputably at a crossroads. The earth has
been an Eden for humans. Our species now confronts the
choice of preserving the paradise or turning it into something far less through overpopulation, pollution and mis-
use. I believe we will stop short of the brink to disaster. We
are obviously an adaptive species and one capable of great
intelligence. Unfortunately, we have a knack for waiting
until the last minute before confronting problems that
threaten our lives or convenience.

A pivotal issue is the value of wilderness and wildlife
to our species. Are there arguments for saving the natural
world that are as strong as those for cleaning up our nest?
We know the dangers of losing the protection of the ozone
layer. We understand that chemical pollution can harm
us. But why is saving the rain forest, the elephant or the
whale important to our lives? What benefit are they to us?
Esoteric, philosophical and ethical reasons for protecting
other life forms are not very persuasive to people struggling to feed their families.

We are late in beginning to think about preserving a
quality of life for the future. Our first task is to reach a
consensus on the goal. From my perspective, our objectives
must include the existence of wilderness and wildlife,
which allow us to satisfy our desire for connection with
the universe and our basic quest for adventure.

The places that I have chosen to look at for this book
are special for their unique wildness; they are unchanged
places that remain essentially as the universe created
them. They are not necessarily the most remote or unpop-
ulated areas that I have had the opportunity to visit. Nor
is their wildness necessarily secure. Some of the places are
ones with which I am quite familiar. Others are places
that I feel I know well because I am so eager to become
better acquainted with them.

The wildest places are not that way just because of
their appearances. They are wild because they embody the
eyes of a tiger, the roar of a lion or the wings of an eagle,
as well as the hot, hanging clouds of the jungle, the pure
ice of the poles or the deep blue waves of the sea. Wildness
is apparent in the moon, the sun and the stars.

This book celebrates the wildness, eternally connected
to the universe, that I saw in the alligator at Mud Creek
and understood in the contented eyes of the bushmen.

Jim Fowler

The Brooks Range thrusts like a scimitar for 600 miles across northern Alaska.

THE FIRST TIME I VISITED THE BROOKS RANGE was in the spring of 1966. A film crew and I were going up to Point Barrow to shoot footage of biologists studying polar bears out on the pack ice.

We left Nome in two Super Cubs. Farther north, as we headed into Kotzebue to refuel, I looked down at frozen Kotzebue Sound and saw a hole about a hundred feet wide in the ice that was filled with white, churning forms. They were beluga whales, more than 20 of them, performing some kind of feeding dance, rising up from below the surface in a circle like a smoke ring, then turning and diving down into the center. The sight was magnificent—unexpected and unforgettable.

As we flew inland over the Brooks Range, I felt like we were entering a vast and absolute wilderness, a world with no human distortion. Below us were row after row of chiseled peaks, remarkably alike in shape, carved by Pleistocene ice and reworked each year by the cycle of thawing and freezing. Dendritic streams, milky with silt, veined their nearly barren flanks.

Somewhere in the heart of the mountains, the plane I was in began running out of fuel. This was a little hair-raising; I breathed easier once we had set down safely on the ridge of a small valley that still had some snow. As the planes skied to a halt, I peered in relief out the window—only to be startled by a herd of caribou that had witnessed our landing. These animals had probably never seen humans before. Unafraid, they gathered around like patrons of a gallery, curious about the odd display of creatures stepping from the bellies of the strange birds. For the 45 minutes that it took us to transfer extra fuel from one Cub to the other, they were our intimates.

Taking off again was tricky because the wind had changed direction, but after a few white-knuckle moments the planes made it back into the air. We stayed low, flying from one valley to the next. With daylight fading, herds of pale Dall sheep were easy to spot against the dark cliffs. We saw golden eagles and more caribou.

We intended to stop in Umiat, an oil exploration camp in the middle of the coastal plain along the Colville River. Once again, though, we had underestimated our fuel consumption. This time, the plane I was in had to set down on a sandbar in the river, southwest of the camp; the other Cub made it all the way to the landing strip. An oil company four-wheeler drove out with some fuel, enough for us to taxi into Umiat. Hopping and skipping from sandbar to sandbar, our plane skimmed along the wide, braided river. Gyrfalcons wheeled before the massive cliffs that wall the banks.

For five days we tried to fly out of Umiat, every time coming back because the planes lost sight of each other in dense fog. Finally, we made it up to Point Barrow, only to discover that the pack ice had broken up early that year. There were plenty of polar bears around, but not a single floe big enough to land on.

We returned to the Brooks Range, having decided to film a biologist studying wolves near Anaktuvuk Pass in what is now Gates of the Arctic National Park. Traveling by dogsled and snowmachine, we tagged along with him as he checked his "trapline." He would immobilize each captured wolf with a tranquilizer, record its data, then attach a radio collar and release it.

One morning a wolf that was not immobilized broke loose. Without thinking, I tackled it, securing it in a headlock with one hand around its muzzle, and hung on for dear life. This was a crocodile-wrestling move that

*Marlin
Perkins had
taught me:
Lassoing a crocodile
would get us exciting
footage of it thrashing
around on the end of
the rope, but the
minute we tried any
manhandling, it
would go limp. The
wolf responded the same
way. It was so surprised to
be tackled by a human that it
just hunkered down and stayed
motionless. We immobilized it, and in
minutes it was sleepy enough to be recorded and collared.*

*We stayed for about a week in the Brooks
Range, filming the biologist as he went about his
work. The sense of enormity, of wide, open spaces
that I had felt on seeing the mountains from the air
was even more intense on the ground. Whenever I came
to a ridgetop, I knew that on the other side awaited only
still wilder country.*

—JF

BROOKS RANGE

BY KIM HEACOX

No connoisseur of the world's great mountains disputes the wonders of the Himalayas, the Andes, the Alps or other famous ranges that crown the continents, anchor cultures and expand the human spirit. "Mountains are the beginning and the end of all natural scenery," extolled Englishman John Ruskin in the mid-1800s. Added John Muir, founder of the Sierra Club in 1892: "Climb the mountains and get their good tidings"—and at his own bidding, climb them he did.

Mountains are no less inspiring today, but they also seem to wince under the ever-tightening pinch of unchecked growth by the human population. Many are becoming more and more painfully crowded.

Imagine, then, a range that is still on the edge of discovery, more remote and less trampled than almost all others; where many of the peaks remain nameless, the valleys peopleless, the rivers boundless; where the map is no longer blank, yet the contour intervals are still wide. Run the range for 600 miles east-west across the top of Alaska, entirely above the Arctic Circle, where time loses meaning in the extremes of 24-hour daylight in summer and 24-hour darkness in winter. Make the range an allegory of age, the weathered peaks not especially tall, yet somehow exotic, largely treeless, often windswept. Finally, name the range for a gifted geologist who explored the terrain of Alaska in the early 1900s: Alfred Hulse Brooks.

One hundred miles north of the Arctic Circle the Koyukuk River threads its way south under the stony watch of Boreal Mountain and Frigid Crags, the twin-peak sentinels known as the "Gates of the Arctic."

This is the Brooks Range. Similes and metaphors fail to apply here; there are few places—indeed, many would say none—*like* the Brooks Range. It is the northernmost chain of continuous mountains in the world. Located at 68° north latitude, more than three times closer to the North Pole than to the Equator, it is an unfettered range interrupted only by a single road and a pipeline, both built during the 1970s to help slake the insatiable thirst for oil in the industrialized United States.

Even for Alaskans, most of whom have never set foot here, the Brooks Range is steeped in fascination. Conjuring up the imagination and desire, it is a landscape of the mind and soul, not just of the map. This is a place of promise, a geography of final hope: for some, the last, best hope for wilderness; for others, the last, best hope for oil.

Here in the arctic ends the Continental Divide that runs up the spines of Mexico, Colorado, Montana and British Columbia, parting rivers that flow to the Beaufort, Chukchi and Bering Seas. Plant communities that flourish in a climb to 10,000 feet in the Rocky Mountains of Colorado tire here at elevations of 2,000 to 4,000 feet, succumbing to the cold, wind and poor soil—the same restrictions on growth imposed by increasing latitude as by higher altitude.

The loftiest peaks in the Brooks Range reach no higher than 10,000 feet, yet they cut impressive vertical profiles, breaking their

After winter-feeding on the forested
southern slopes, caribou migrate hundreds
of miles to reach their summer calving
grounds on the northern tundra along the
Beaufort Sea.

A forage-fattened caribou bull stands
in the Kobuk Valley, the velvet covering
of its bloodied antlers torn after rubbing
against trees.

With intoxicating effect and defiance of scale, an unnamed valley north of the arctic divide blends delicate details of color, shape and texture with distant expanses of windswept mountains, sky and clouds.

backs against the brooding arctic skies at the northern limits of the continent. The granite fangs of the Arrigetch Peaks and the ice-cut Romanzof Mountains in the heart of the range are among the most breathtaking pinnacles in this part of the world.

Ironically, most of arctic Alaska receives a yearly average of less than 10 inches of precipitation, and is therefore technically a desert. Yet, the signatures of ice and water are everywhere in the Brooks Range: Glaciers punctuate the mountains, rivers wind their way through the valleys, and countless lakes and meltwater pools dot the open lowlands of the north slope and coastal plain. How can there be so much water in a veritable desert? Evaporation is minimal, and most of the underlying ground is locked in permafrost, a matrix of ice and rock that penetrates down from just below the surface to a depth of as much as 2,000 feet. In summer, the upper crust of permafrost melts into a tapestry of tundra and water.

Contradictions rule the Brooks Range. Bush pilots speak of weather that is at once magical and mercurial. Hikers encounter fogs that sweep in from the Beaufort Sea, dropping the temperature 20 degrees and leaving them disoriented or even lost. River rafters follow channels that are sometimes flanked by vertical walls of ice up to 10 feet high, thrust without notice into chasms of beauty and danger the likes of which they have never experienced.

FAR LEFT: *The flare of autumn fires the leaves of bearberry on Boreal Mountain.* NEAR LEFT: *A fleece-draped musk ox ruefully tolerates a horde of tormenting insects.*

Other than the expectant mothers, who den on the northern shores in winter, polar bears camp on ice packs off the coast.

When Robert Marshall, hiker *bon vivant* and co-founder of The Wilderness Society, lived and traveled in the arctic wilds during the 1920s and 1930s, he envisioned the entire Brooks Range as a single, vast reserve stretching from the mountains north to the coast of the Beaufort Sea. Taking this dream back with him to New York City and Washington, D.C., he was once asked, "How much wilderness do we need?" He replied, "How many Brahms symphonies do we need?"

Marshall championed a gallant fight, but the United States government at the time was embroiled in other pressing matters. Forty years after he died, however, more than three-quarters of the Brooks Range was granted protection within the boundaries of four federal conservation units: the 19-million-acre Arctic National Wildlife Refuge in the east; the 8.4-million-acre Gates of the Arctic National Park and Preserve in the center; the 6.5-million-acre Noatak National Preserve and 1.7-million-acre Kobuk Valley National Park in the west.

Combined, these four areas are larger than Pennsylvania—an abrupt end to their similarity since nearly the entire Brooks Range is pristine wilderness. Six rivers that have been officially designated wild and

Timber wolves, formidable predators, linger at the carcass of a vanquished prey.

scenic flow through Gates of the Arctic alone. The slopes and summits of most vistas here have seldom, if ever, felt the tread of human feet; rather than inviting the breaking of first ground, they thrill because first ground remains unbroken.

Flying over the Brooks Range in winter numbs the mind with the specter of a frozen, snow-covered and windswept world. Indeed, few places can be so inhospitable. The air settles down with a grip as cold as iron, and plunges in temperature to -50°F. are common. Yet beneath this icy veneer lies a dormant land waiting to burst with life, as it does with the returning sun every spring.

Summer finds the tundra splashed with wildflowers, such as saxifrage, moss campion, phlox, avens and arnica. Birds arrive from as far away as Russia, Japan, Tasmania, California, and Central and South America to nest on the tundra. Tracks of grizzly bears trace the rivers and add dimension to the land; these bears suddenly loom in the imagination, and could be anywhere. Grayling rise in the rivers. Wolves howl from afar, or are they near? Musk ox, looking like shaggy cousins of Pleistocene beasts, stand their ground on the open tundra. And Dall sheep, the only wild, white species of sheep in the

OVERLEAF: The snow-sloughing, black-granite peaks of Arrigetch, Inuit for "fingers of the hand extended," thrust skyward as if to taunt.

A molting willow ptarmigan, not yet fully white-plumed for the winter, emits a raucous warning call that sounds like "Go back! Go back! Go back!"

world, graze the alpine slopes. Midnight shafts of cinnabar sunlight streak the mountains, and a sky that dances with northern lights in winter is now, in June, painted in pastels of pink and orange. A lone fox might pass with an arctic ground squirrel clamped in its jaws, failing to see the Baird's sandpiper, the horned lark or the ruddy turnstone that sits motionless nearby on its nest.

More than 200 species of birds have been recorded in the Brooks Range and on the north slope and coastal plain where vast wetlands of tundra, twisted rivers, snow-fed pools and lakes spill from the crest of the mountains to the sea. Nearly half of these species breed here every summer, and for some—ravens, snowy owls, ptarmigan and gyrfalcons—this place is a year-round home.

Yet, if there is one animal that embodies arctic Alaska and the Brooks Range, it is the caribou. Called the "nomads of the north," the caribou are to this part of the world what wildebeests are to East Africa and bison once were to the Great Plains of North America. They move together by the tens of thousands as if they made up a single, magnificent organism. Like a migrating lifeblood, they course through the valleys and pulsate across the rivers to the rhythms of an ancient, arctic metronome that only they appear to understand. Unpredictable landscapes are said to breed unpredictable animals and, taking the word of the Inuit, "Only the wind knows the ways of the caribou."

Three distinct, major herds dwell in the region: the western arctic, the central arctic

Wisps of white bell heather lace tundra in the Arctic National

At Onion Portage, 40 miles north of the
Arctic Circle, sunrise spills over the Jade
Mountains and onto the Kobuk River.

*Like a pink refrain to the stanzas of summer,
phlox burst into chorus on the coastal plain.*

For more than ten thousand years the native peoples of arctic and subarctic Alaska have hunted caribou for meat, clothing and tools. As if in spiritual union with the land, they leave almost no part of the animals to waste. This has been the custom, "the way," in villages from Kaktovik and Umiat in the north to Anaktuvuk Pass and Arctic Village in the heart of the mountains and to Alatna, Kobuk and Ambler in the south. Villagers today travel by snowmachine in winter and by boat in summer, shooting caribou as they bound through the snow or swim the rivers. The variation on an ancient way of life, called "subsistence living" by biologists, bureaucrats and natives alike, is carried on in much of arctic Alaska, including the national parks, preserves and refuges in the Brooks Range. For better or worse, the modern world has arrived with internal-combustion engines and high-powered rifles, as well as television, chocolate and 80-proof whiskey.

The vanguard of change dates back to the 1800s when European explorers were searching for the fabled Northwest Passage. White men and natives were equally aston-

*the summer dress of alpine
Wildlife Refuge.*

and the Porcupine—so-named after the Yukon river where this herd winters. Over the last two decades all three herds have grown in number, most dramatically the western arctic, up from 75,000 in the 1970s to 500,000. But population cycles for the caribou seem to be the rule rather than the exception, and biologists expect the size of the herds to decline in the future. The caribou roam by necessity, for a herd that lingers too long in one location risks overgrazing. Near the turn of the century explorer Knud Rasmussen wrote: "Sometimes the caribou migration in June is so enormous...the animals are three days in passing a village; the whole country is alive, and one can see neither the beginning nor the end—the whole earth seems to be moving."

As the snows retreat in the spring, sandpipers flock to the tundra of the north slope to court, mate and nest.

ished by each other, and the natives of arctic Alaska, like those of Greenland, no doubt asked the white men, "Where do you come from, the sun or the moon?" By the early 1900s gold seekers were picking their way through the Brooks Range in hopes of finding veins as rich as those in Juneau, Nome and the Klondike—only to be disappointed.

The latest chapter of change pivots on oil, the black gold of industrial America, and began in earnest in February of 1968. Oil-soaked sands were found 8,700 feet below the tundra of the north slope at Prudhoe Bay, along the arctic coast about 130 miles from the crest of the Brooks Range. Industry came like it never had before. Construction included the North Slope Haul Road, now called the Dalton Highway, and the 800-mile-long Trans-Alaska Pipeline from Prudhoe Bay to Valdez at Prince William Sound, which was completed in 1977.

By 1992 over seven billion barrels of oil had flowed to Valdez for shipment south, providing the United States with 25 percent of its domestic supply. Reserves were declining, however, and industry set its sights 65 miles east of Prudhoe Bay, on the coastal plain of the Arctic National Wildlife Refuge, where the promise of oil was again tempting. Statistical assessments yielded a mid-range estimate of about eight percent of the national supply by the turn of the century.

But would the United States—home to the five percent of the world's population

At Boreal Mountain along the north fork of the Koyukuk River, the first oils of autumn's brush color the landscape by August.

that consumes 25 percent of the world's energy—persist in putting wilderness at risk for development? Battle lines were drawn and arguments sharpened. The oil lobby insisted no sacrifice was necessary, that modern technology would mitigate environmental impacts and provide for safe development along with needed jobs. Conservationists countered with the charge that environmentally safe development was oxymoronic when applied to wilderness, that fuel efficiency standards should be raised and alternative energy sources pursued.

The Brooks Range along with the north slope and coastal plain, through which the caribou move in concert with the land, has been heralded as "the smile on the Mona Lisa" and the "American Serengeti." Yet for all its remoteness and ruggedness, the place is very much of this world, balanced on the heavy anvil of humanity and still on the feathered edge of discovery, illuminated by desire and defined by open space. The riches of the region cannot be measured in mere commodities of gold and oil; they are to be found in the spiritual tonic of wilderness where souls are free to spread out with the land. As writer Robert Marshall wrote in his book *Alaska Wilderness*, "...no comfort, no security, no invention, no brilliant thought which the modern world had to offer could provide half the elation of the days spent in the little explored, uninhabited world of the arctic wilderness."

*A*N OPPORTUNITY TO STUDY THE HARPY EAGLE brought me to this wilderness region of South America in 1959. Since childhood I have been fascinated by birds of prey, and the harpy, known as "the flying wolf of the Amazon," was of particular interest because it is the largest eagle in the world. Full-grown members of this species have wingspans as wide as seven feet.

From Georgetown in Guyana, we flew to an isolated outpost in the rain forest near the Brazilian border, just north of the Equator. I began showing around photos of a harpy to find out if anyone had ever seen such a bird. A young Amerindian led me on a hike to a 200-foot-tall silk cotton tree; nearly halfway up it was a harpy nest about seven feet in diameter. For two weeks I literally camped out at the tree, observing and filming. The nest was the first ever found and studied in the wild by a scientist.

Some Brazilian vaqueros invited me along to hunt for diamonds about a hundred miles north on the Ireng River in the Guiana Highlands. I agreed to go, but my interest was in finding harpies and anacondas among the tepuis, the unusual, flat-topped mountains of sandstone found in this part of the world. We ended up at Sierra Pacaraima a little southwest of Mount Roraima, tallest of the tepuis.

One day a couple of Amerindians came through our camp with a huge anaconda tied up in leather lassos on the back of a bullock cart. The snake weighed about 300 pounds and was as big around as a nail keg. We put the sluggish-looking reptile into an underground bunker I had built where the temperature would stay constant.

With a little arm-twisting, I convinced a reluctant photographer, who was terrified of snakes, to shoot a film sequence of the anaconda. As I reached into the bunker to grab the snake's head, it bit my hand and held on. I had never before felt a grip of such pressure and strength. An anaconda has about two hundred hollow, inch-long teeth, which it uses like grappling hooks to hold onto the prey that it suffocates.

When the snake began to wrap me, I became really worried: An anaconda of such size would have no trouble crushing my rib cage and suffocating me. Grabbing its tail, I pulled the snake into the open. Then, I fell down and the anaconda swallowed my arm up to the shoulder. My two local guides ran off in fright into the forest. The photographer was white with shock. He was not even filming my predicament!

But the anaconda must have thought I was too big to swallow. Once I had somehow managed to relax and stop struggling, the snake gave up on wrapping me. As I tried to pry open its powerful jaws, the anaconda gradually relaxed its grip on my arm. I was lucky. I got off with only a minor bacterial infection and a punctured arm that was useless for five days.

A few weeks later I set off to find harpies near a tepui east of Mount Roraima. As I combed the forest one day, capuchin monkeys suddenly fell from the trees, smacking down on the ground like ripe apples. One landed near me, then crawled under a root and tried to hide in the leaves. As I got down on my knees to approach the monkey, I heard a strange whooshing sound and turned around to look straight into the eyes of an adult female harpy that sat on a branch not 20 feet away. She had been hunting the capuchins. As long as I stayed on my knees the eagle showed no sign of fear, but as soon as I stood up she flew off. Getting so close to that harpy was a thrill that I will never forget.

—JF

A remote sentinel 9,094 feet high at the intersecting borders of Venezuela, Guyana and Brazil, Mount Roraima is the tallest summit in a range of unusual flat-topped, sandstone mountains.

RORAIMA

BY GREG STOTT

Charged with reassessing a list of the world's great natural wonders, a forum of scholarly gentlemen gathered at a London salon in the 1860s. Mount Everest, the Grand Canyon and the recently discovered Victoria Falls were among the sites that met with general approval. "And what about Mount Roraima in Venezuela?" someone asked. There was an uncomfortable silence. Then came a disdainful suggestion that perhaps not enough was yet known about the frontiers of South America.

The response was narrow-minded and, as time would reveal, utterly wrong-headed. No more than a pinprick on an atlas, Mount Roraima stands sentinel to remote, little-explored corners of Venezuela, Guyana and Brazil. At 9,094 feet, the mountain is the tallest in a chain of more than a hundred flat-topped peaks that rise like tropical sky islands from a deeply eroded, 200,000-square-mile plateau called La Gran Sabana, or "the Great Savanna." A veritable wilderness paradise, this sheer-walled, 25-square-mile colossus of rock in the middle of the South American rain forest would seem to most people to qualify easily as a natural marvel.

In the dialect of the local natives, the name of the mountain is Ru-ruima, meaning "Mother of the Waters." This reputation stems from the almost-constant rains of April through November, when the region becomes one of the wettest places in the world. Thick, gray rain clouds swirl over the pill-box summit, creating thunderous waterfalls that cascade off it in all directions.

Some of the torrents that spill from the ancient sandstone cliffs rush north to the Orinoco River. Other waters flow northeast to the lowlands of Guyana, and still others pour south into the mighty Amazon basin, eventually to flow to the Atlantic Ocean some 900 miles to the southeast.

Of the thousands of waterfalls that come to ground in La Gran Sabana, none is quite as spectacular as Angel Falls. Cascading uninterrupted 3,212 feet down a mist-laden escarpment, the waters of this great cataract plunge about 20 times the distance of North America's Niagara Falls and some seven times further than Zambia's Victoria Falls.

There are many other natural wonders in this vast highland. The table mountains—tepuis in the dialect of the local natives—contain some of the oldest rock on earth. The weathered sandstone, a vestige of the Pleistocene epoch and the landforms that existed long before plants and animals ever evolved, is thought to be as much as two billion years old—about half the age of the planet itself.

Ever since the prehistoric land split into the continents of South America and Africa, the primal landscape of La Gran Sabana has been worn away by natural forces of erosion. Over the past 70 million years the softer portions of the sandstone have been removed, leaving behind the diamond-tough, quartzite

Flashing defensive colors distasteful to its would-be predators, a leaf-footed bug wanders boldly across some foliage.

*At Canaima National Park, the tannin-dyed waters
of the Carrao River spill over Hacha Falls.*

tepuis that appear from a distance to loom like the frozen waves of some ancient sea.

Although early explorers of this grizzled region came to pan the waters for gold, the real mother lode of the tepuis was in the flora and fauna. As many as half of the plant varieties and a quarter of the animals of Mount Roraima exist nowhere else in the world; some of them have only recently been discovered and classified.

So far, botanists have identified more than 900 types of orchids that flourish in La Gran Sabana; together, these flowers account for close to a tenth of the region's vegetation. As many as 60 different varieties, some of them ground-hugging bloomers of minute proportions, may inhabit a single acre of ground. Appropriately, an orchid called the mayflower is Venezuela's national flower.

In the dense jungle, there are delicate ferns and spiky, water-filled bromeliads that were unknown to the outside world only a few decades ago. On isolated plateaus, there are insect-eating pitcher plants that are taller than humans. Living close by is a highly unusual species of pygmy frog, whose eggs are not hatched in water and whose young do not follow the usual pattern of developing from tadpoles to full-grown adults. These frogs neither hop nor swim.

Here, just a few degrees north of the Equator, bleak, twisted faces of rock look onto patches of mosses, lichens and fungi that cling to ground flushed of nutrients by the torrential rains. Not far off, the washed-away soils collect to nurture the lush, tropical jungle that is also characteristic of the area. Although the most accessible sites of La Gran Sabana have been scoured by botanists, entomologists and other scientists, much of the region remains unprobed, filled with the promise of yet additional discoveries.

Attempts by outside explorers to uncover the mysteries of this part of the world go back as far as 1595, when Sir Walter Raleigh organized an expedition into the interior of present-day Guyana. His mission was to claim territory for Great Britain and to locate

The meandering Carrao River flows across a stretch of La Gran Sabana within view of two distant tepuis.

El Dorado, a mythical land of wealth. In his quest, he made what was probably the first sighting of the tepuis by a European.

Reporting on one of the impressive summits, Raleigh wrote: "I was enformed of the mountain of Christall...we saw it farre off and it appeared like a white church towre of an exceeding height. There falleth over it a mightie river which toucheth no parte of the side of the mountaine, but rusheth over the top of it, and falleth to the grounde with terrible noyse and clamor, as if 1,000 great belles were knockt one against another. I think there is not in the world so strange an overfall, not so wonderful to behold."

There were few other foreign incursions on this land for more than two centuries. In 1838, however, German-born scientist Robert Schomburgk explored the region for Great Britain's Royal Geographical Society. His arduous trek lasted months and took him to the base of Mount Roraima, but he left without finding a route to the top.

On his return to England, Schomburgk wrote: "According to the traditions of the Indians, the summits of the flat-topped gigantic sandstone walls which never can be reached by human beings, contain large lakes, full of remarkable fish-like dolphins, and are continually encircled by gigantic white eagles—their eternal warders."

Schomburgk's delivery of exotic plant specimens, along with his tales of a lofty, invincible vault soaring into the clouds

Dagger-leafed herbs crowd a soggy niche.

From a gash in the sheer face of Auyan Tepui, giant Angel Falls plummets down a 3,212-foot escarpment.

fanned the imaginations of those hearing his reports. Calling the distant Mount Roraima "one of the greatest marvels and mysteries," a correspondent for *The Spectator*, a popular journal of the day, implored his 1877 readers: "Will no one explore Roraima and bring us back the tidings which it has been waiting these thousands of years to give us?"

At least one individual, travel writer J.W. Boddam-Whetham, took up the challenge, but Mount Roraima turned him away too. "We most assuredly failed to tear the veil from the head of this mysterious Sphinx," he wrote in his 1879 book, *Roraima and British Guiana.* "I do not think it possible to make the ascent of Roraima except by a balloon."

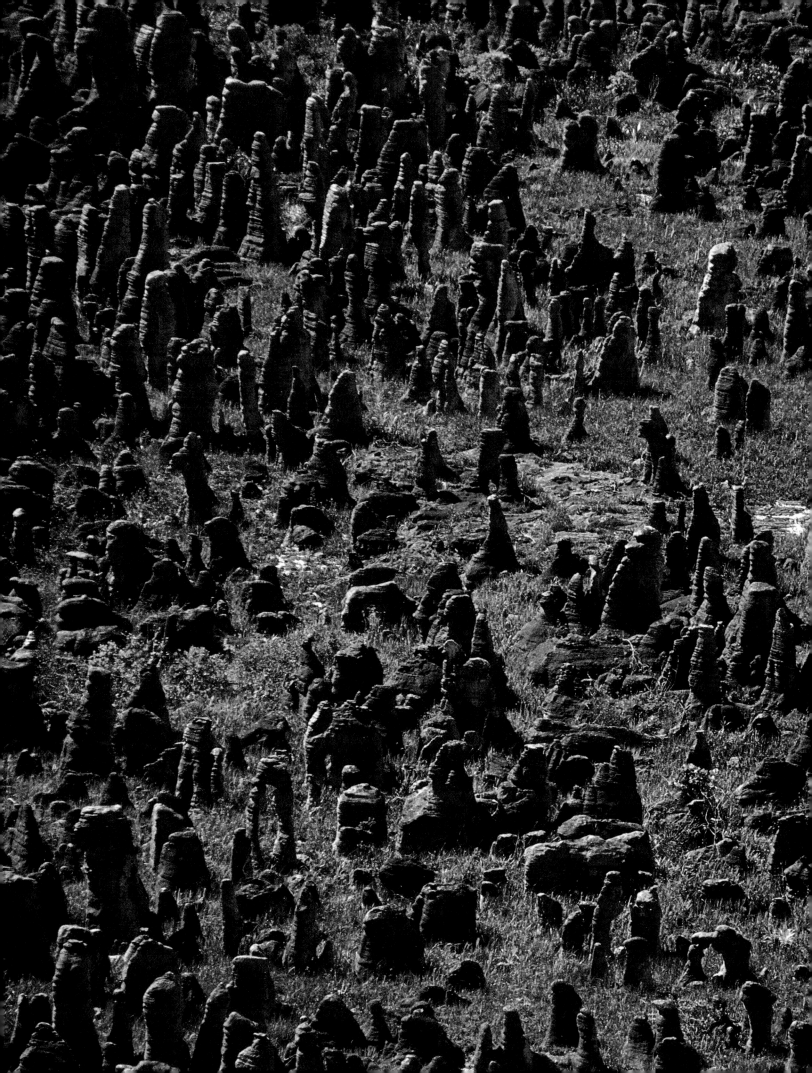

Other scribes of the time added melodrama to the allure of Mount Roraima by suggesting that the truncated top might just be the domain of prehistoric animals. Some even postulated that dinosaurs and the like might be suspended in their evolutionary development on the unreachable roof.

Discovering the facts fell to Everard Im Thurn, a British botanist and magistrate, who in 1884 found a route to the elusive crown of Roraima along the slippery bed of a stream. The fabled mountain offered no prehistoric creatures, he informed the outside world, but it did hold a trove of undiscovered flora and fauna. He described the windblown summit, as others have since, as a rather barren but sensual place, filled with corrugated rocks, deep chasms and caves, and sinkholes that plunge hundreds of feet.

Legions of people were fascinated by Im Thurn's riveting accounts—one of them Sir Arthur Conan Doyle. Although he never actually came to the region, the renowned creator of Sherlock Holmes was inspired to write *The Lost World*, the fictional tale of an eccentric named Professor Challenger, who finds an unknown colony of dinosaurs isolated atop a mountain in South America.

But while Professor Challenger and his Paleozoic beasts were the products of wishful thinking, Mount Roraima presides over a region that is indeed home to some fascinating and forbidding creatures. Among them are two species of ponerine ants. Members of the family known as *Dinoponera grandis* can grow up to two inches long; they are the largest ants in the world. Another type, the *Paraponera*, is smaller, but its sting can paralyze or kill a human.

Great natural protectors of the wilderness, life-threatening snakes, scorpions, and tarantulas and other spiders also do their part to keep all but the most adventuresome away from La Gran Sabana. English mountaineer John Streetly told of a harrowing encounter that he experienced in a grove of trees while on a reconnaissance expedition to Mount Roraima in 1973. "I saw a coiled bushmaster, its head raised to thigh level ready to strike at my right leg as it swung past the sapling. Lethargy disappeared in a flash and swinging to the left, I knocked Renton [a native guide] flying, avoiding what must have been an almost definite fatality from the seven-foot snake." Later the same year, as Streetly's colleagues made a grueling first

ascent of the so-called Prow, a sheer wall overhanging the northeast face of Mount Roraima, the team of climbers were astonished by the great numbers of scorpions and tarantulas that stood in their way.

Two other adventurers who came to the region a decade later left with their own chilling tale. As writer J.M. Ridden and his wife Christine prepared to enter a swimming hole on the grassy savanna, their guide spotted an "undulating form with a mighty triangular head, small neck and fat body." The slithering creature turned out to be a bathing water boa that Ridden estimated to be about 18 feet long and two feet in circumference.

Such narrow brushes with danger are an unavoidable fact of life in the tropical climate of La Gran Sabana. But none of the perils are enough to dispel the exotic allure of Mount Roraima; indeed, they seem only to heighten the romantic appeal of this once lost world.

The 20th century's fascination with the region was given a boost by the exploits of a colorful American bush pilot named Jimmy Angel. Recruited out of Panama in 1936, Angel flew a mining engineer deep into the Venezuelan interior on a quest for gold. Unlike many of their predecessors who had searched and left with empty sacks, Angel claimed that he and his partner had actually struck it rich, collecting some 75 pounds of the precious metal in just a few days along the banks of a remote river.

Foliage mimicry by a clever dead-leaf mantis helps the insect to stay inconspicuous.

However, when Angel returned with his wife and a friend in 1937, he failed to find the river site. In making a bold landing on Auyan Tepui he lost his plane, which settled into the marshy ground. But during this visit he discovered the great cascading waters that today bear his name: Angel Falls. Angel's plane remained mired in the mud of the tepui until 1970, when the Venezuelan Air Force hauled it out with a helicopter for installation in an aeronautical museum. There, the plane sits as a reminder of one man's daring.

Unfortunately, the popular lore of La Gran Sabana comes with a downside for the wilderness region. With the rise in its reputation, Mount Roraima has attracted growing numbers of adventure-seeking travelers. Such interest notwithstanding, the route to the tallest of the tepuis can still be arduous. A

A tree-climbing passiflora opens slender-petaled blossoms of passionate red.

OVERLEAF: *The name of its species understandably derived from "hairy cat," a disheveled-looking caterpillar munches on a leaf.*

A young collared peccary hunts for grubs and small vertebrates, supplementing a chiefly vegetarian diet.

dirt road that links Venezuela's capital of Caracas with the Brazilian city of Manaus in the Amazon region passes within 30 miles of Mount Roraima. Rutted and bumpy at the best of times, the road is sometimes unpassable in the rainy season, even with a four-wheeled drive vehicle.

Even so, parts of the region have become pockmarked with the scars of campfires. Sinkholes and shallow valleys atop the much-climbed tepuis have had their magnificent reserves of quartz crystals looted by visitors.

Valleys and canyons better protected by the chiseled topography of the tepuis still hold bedazzling oceans of crystals. But for how long? No nook or cranny of the tepuis can be considered too remote to be beyond the reach of would-be pillagers.

Such threats to the integrity of the region have been recognized by the Venezuelan government. Much of La Gran Sabana and a vast

An ocelot, agile climber of trees, appears ready to leap from a horizontal limb.

Lured by the scent only to be trapped among the hairs, insects drown in the sun pitcher, which will consume them as food.

adjacent area to the west have been set aside as Canaima National Park—a promising step toward protecting the wilderness. But a staff of only a half-dozen people has been hired to oversee the region and the number of annual visitors is expected to rise to 40,000.

Moreover, the Venezuelan hydroelectric utility has provoked a heated debate with its plans to build five dams on the Caroni River, one of the watersheds that flow through La Gran Sabana and drain into the Orinoco River. One of the principal environmental concerns is that a portion of this timeless landscape may be flooded in the process.

High atop Mount Roraima, accessible only by a rigorous climb, there is the reward of a sweeping panorama of what seems to be an unspoiled corner of the world. Dwellings and sites of proposed dams are beyond sight. The unlikely appearance of a human below would seem to be no more than a speck on a

firmament that is utterly invincible. However formidable though, La Gran Sabana is no match for the unstoppable force of human disregard. A singularly diverse landscape, the region enjoys an advantage of geography, but not immunity to destruction.

La Gran Sabana, like other wilderness regions, merits preservation. Some reasons for protecting such a resource involve complicated logic about the long-term best interests of humans. One argument, for example, is that a plant or animal unique to this habitat may some day yield the cure to a world-threatening disease.

Other reasons are simpler. One of them can be found in the words of British mountaineer Hamish MacInnes. After he had climbed Mount Roraima in 1973, MacInnes wrote: "It was a wonderland like nothing on earth. For me, Roraima is still one of the wonders of the world."

Jagged, glacial peaks of Torres del Paine catch the evening's golden light.

ON A PLANE TO TIERRA DEL FUEGO IN 1991,
I became forever spellbound by this isolated
region in the southern Andes. A breathtaking landscape
of ice-capped peaks, forests, small lakes and scruffy plains,
Torres del Paine National Park is named for the mountain towers that are its most distinctive feature. Curious
geological sandwiches of white granite wedged between
layers of gray shale, the sheer summits were not climbed
until the middle of this century.

Because the park contains many different habitats,
there is great variety in the wildlife. Guanacos, vicuñas,
pumas, Geoffroy's cats, pudús and gray foxes are among
the dozens of types of mammals found in the area. There
are also hundreds of species of birds—everything from
flamingos, swans and ibises to meadow larks, Magellanic
woodpeckers and ostrich-like Darwin's rheas.

One colossal bird, the Andean condor, first brought
me to this part of the world in 1968. I was participating in
a study on the territorial range of the condor, an endeavor
that involved fitting some of the birds with radio transmitters so their movements could be tracked. My goal was
also to find an active nest. Condors usually raise their
young in caves at sites not easily reached by humans, and
no scientist at the time had been known to have studied
an active nest.

As I went about my work, I was being shadowed by
an Andean Indian named Tomás. I eventually learned
that his boss, the operator of a copper mine, thought we
were trapping condors for sale to zoos and fitting them
with radio transmitters in order to locate mineral
deposits—gold, to be specific. Wanting a piece of the

Named for the pinnacled towers of granite
it surrounds, Torres del Paine National Park
encompasses 935 square miles of varied-
habitat wilderness in southern Chile's
portion of Patagonia.

action, the boss had dispatched Tomás to keep an eye on the progress we made.

Once the misconceptions were corrected, Tomás and I got along fine. One day he invited me to a spot along the coast where he knew there was a condor nest. I had just gotten word that researchers from the University of Wisconsin had discovered a condor nest in the Colombian Andes. However, no one had thought that condors would nest so close to the ocean.

Tomás directed me to a 400-foot cliff on Chile's northern coastline. I put on my harness, tied my thick nylon rope to the bumper of our pickup truck—parked well back from the crumbling edge—and prepared to rappel the cliff. Tomás pulled out of his sack a rope of braided guanaco hair—one that I would not have used to climb down stairs. But he hammered a spike into a rock and tied off, then went down hand-over-hand 20 feet to a ledge about four feet wide.

After I had joined him on the ledge, I watched in amazement as he untied his rope, sauntered off 40 feet along the ledge and disappeared around a corner.

He returned with a big smile on his face—he had found the cave.

The rocks above us were so jagged that I had to tie off as well, and I decided to show Tomás how to belay me. I suspected that if I fell he might not be able to hold me, but the thought that I was anchored gave me the security I needed to walk the ledge. Confident that he understood what he was to do, I inched along until the ledge narrowed to about two feet and an overhang obliged me almost to crawl. Then, I froze. There I was: clinging to a shelf of crumbly rock hundreds of feet above the crashing sea, too terrified to move forward or backward.

Hearing something behind me, I glanced over my shoulder and there was Tomás, another big smile on his face. He had been dutifully following me along the ledge, picking up the rope as he went. Gone was any semblance of rational safety procedures, and I found my predicament so absurd that I had to laugh. As I did, my fright evaporated. I rounded the corner to where the ledge widened and there, a few feet above me, was the cave.

There was only one additional problem: Tomás had neglected to tell me that a few days earlier the chicks had been taken from the nest. I had just risked my life to reach an empty hole! The fragments of egg shells I found, however, were evidence that condors do nest on coastal cliffs.

The study on the range of the condor, however, was thoroughly successful. To my surprise, condors were found to range all along the coast from Tierra del Fuego to Peru. Our work confirmed that condors reside along the coastal deserts of the north, and that many condors make daily round-trips of up to 150 miles, flying between nests in the mountains and feeding grounds along the sea.

To this day, though, no one has claimed credit for finding an active condor nest in Torres del Paine. Having this honor can be one of my incentives for returning to the wilds of southern Chile.

—JF

TORRES DEL PAINE

BY PAT & BAIBA MORROW

Rising from the flat, desolate plains known as the pampas, rows of granite mountains stand defiantly in the face of howling winds. Apart from these ice-helmeted giants, only the solitary condor with its mighty ten-foot wingspan dares confront the gale. Whipped by gusts into a foamy froth, the waters of Lago de Grey catch mammoth blocks of glacial ice that crash down from the surrounding peaks. Odd though it may sound, this is just another summer's day in Chile's Torres del Paine National Park.

In this weather-beaten wilderness of Patagonia at the southern extremity of South America, nature unleashes meteorological forces that roil combatively—whatever the season. Skirting the ice-mined waters that envelop Antarctica, the Pacific and Atlantic Oceans collide at Cape Horn, propelling the huge air masses they carry into onshore confrontation. So constant are the winds that locals jokingly offer a simple way for adventuring newcomers to experience this part of the world: Just stand still and everything will eventually blow past.

Like the armor-clad armadillo that wanders the rugged landscape, the region seems thick-skinned and insensitive, numbed by the almost-constant inclemency. Anything that falters here is said to be ruthlessly swept away by la escoba de Dios, "the broom of God." Warm, sunny weather is rare. Even on New Year's Day, the height of the austral summer, there is the possibility of snow.

Defined by geography rather than by political boundaries, Patagonia stretches 1,000 miles north from the archipelago of Tierra del Fuego and takes in the entire southern mainland of Chile and Argentina. Encompassing some 260,000 square miles of wild terrain, the region exceeds the combined areas of California and Oregon. Much of the landscape is unnervingly monotonous and dreary.

Although characterized by extremes of topography and climate, this remote corner of the southern hemisphere was not named for any of its natural attributes. Curiously, the name Patagonia stems from an early variety of native footwear. In 1520 the Portuguese explorer Ferdinand Magellan landed near what is now Punta Arenas, along the strait that bears his name. There, he met local Tehuelche Indians, who wore oversized moccasins made from the hide of the guanaco, a humpless cousin of the camel. As the story goes, Magellan is said to have dubbed the region "patagones," from a Spanish word for "big feet."

Within this "land of tempest"—a later, perhaps more apt description by British explorer and mountaineer Eric Shipton—sits the 935-square-mile wilderness reserve called Torres del Paine National Park. Huddled in the southern fringes of the 4,500-mile-long Andes, the park is about 240 miles north of Punta Arenas, the southernmost city in the world. A once-thriving port that went into

Under constant assault from the winds off the open pampas, a stooped lenga tree flails limbs disfigured by the incessant blowing.

decline with the opening of the Panama Canal in 1914, Punta Arenas is the jumping-off point for most travelers to the park.

On the sprawling pampas and rolling foothills between this town and Torres del Paine, mustachioed cowboys, called gauchos or huasos, ride on horseback as they tend herds of sheep that number in the thousands. The ranches, or estancias, stretch out over vast expanses of land. About an acre of range is needed to support a single sheep. Although they are shorn of their protective cloak of wool only once a year, the sheep must be sheltered in sheds in order to survive the frequent, violent storms.

On occasion, the doleful monotony of the landscape is interrupted by a flock of flightless, ostrich-like birds called Darwin's rheas, or ñandús. Comically flapping their ineffectual wings, they dart helter-skelter across the fields, kicking up thick clouds of dust with their powerful, scaly legs. But the ungainly appearance of the ñandús is deceptive. They are well suited for even the roughest terrain and can outrun a horse.

As if without warning to the visitor, striking stone towers loom suddenly on the horizon. The profiles of the mountains are no less impressive than they were in 1945 when, after 30 years of exploring Patagonia, the Salesian missionary priest Padre Agostini wrote: "The Paine massif is unrivalled...like an impregnable fortress, crowned with towers, pinnacles and monstrous horns surging boldly to the sky. In its colours and form it is without doubt one of the most fantastic

ABOVE, LEFT: *A family of upland geese scout a stretch of lakeshore.* ABOVE: *Two ashy-headed geese picnic on the pampas grasses.*

A pair of coscoroba swans guide their chicks across the shallows of a small lake.

*Perhaps sensing danger to
the grazing herd, a guanaco
interrupts its meal to scan
the horizon.*

*A European hare that detects a predator often
halts and remains motionless, hoping to be
passed unnoticed.*

and spectacular sights that human imagination can conceive."

Although the mountains are not big by Andean standards, they make up in drama what they lack in stature. While few peaks in the Torres del Paine rise higher than 8,500 to 9,000 feet, they are so sheer and steep that none of them were successfully scaled until the 1950s.

Paine Grande stands tallest at 10,007 feet. Glacier remnants cling to its shoulders and a rooster-like comb of wind-brushed snow graces the jagged ridge at its summit. Equally splendid are the twin horns of Cuernos del Paine. Composed mainly of pinkish-gray granite and crowned with a layer of coal-black shale, they rear majestically before the churning rapids of a river called Salto Chico.

The stunning batholiths of Torres del Paine are the remains of tectonic upheavals that drove the southern continents apart mil-

lions of years ago. Beginning as fingers of molten rock extruded through cracks in the earth's crust, the spires were carved over many eons by glacial ice that removed the softer stone encasing them.

Local legend, however, puts a different spin on these geologic developments. Long, long ago, so the story goes, an evil serpent named Cai Cai brought about a flood to rid the land of humans. When the waters receded, Cai Cai found the bodies of some warriors who had perished and turned them to stone, thereby creating the towers. The wailing, mournful winds common to the area are said to be the voices of Cai Cai's victims.

Sadly, indigenous people of this region were victimized in other ways. Entire native communities of Patagonia and Tierra del Fuego were decimated in the years following the arrival of European settlers, wiped out by guns and previously unknown diseases. Few

OVERLEAF: *The ice-capped granite twins of Cuernos del Paine rise boldly to the rear of shimmering blue lakes lined with glacial silt.*

Green blankets of moss drape broad-shouldered granite outcroppings along the rugged foothills.

LEFT: *Flame-red blooms light up a Chilean fire bush.*
NEAR RIGHT: *The delectable shape of its flowers betrays the climbing sweet pea.*
FAR RIGHT: *A pair of yellow calceolaria blooms open up like eager mouths.*

traces remain of the original inhabitants, although tribal names such as Tehuelche, Ona, Yahgan and Alacaluf are still attached to the land.

Paine, pronounced "pie-nay," is usually translated as "pink." The word is believed to have been derived from the dialect of the Tehuelche. It was used to name the towers, which take on a rosy-tinged gleam when exposed to the shining sun. English-speaking adventurers have been less charitable, however, nicknaming the mountains the "Towers of Pain." In a good month, there may be three days when the tops are not shrouded by clouds.

Nevertheless, the commanding profiles of the rock towers are impossible to ignore. They are heart and soul to this wild region, visible from most vantage points in the park: the clean-cut South, Central and North Towers behind Cuernos; the fierce, neighboring ramparts called the Fortress, the Sword and the Blade; the looming walls of Fitzroy and Cerro Torre, 200 miles to the north in Argentina.

Like the ice-topped monoliths that are the park's landmarks, every element of this wilderness emanates an oddly fickle austerity. The winds, although biting, seem also to beckon; they are the siren song of a seductive deceiver. The lakes are a haunting marriage of Cimmerian gloom and enchanting color. Even as the waters impassively mirror the cold stone of the towers around them,

they embellish features of the rocky faces with the brilliant shades of Chile's native gemstones: lapis lazuli and malachite. Lago Pehoé, one of the many lakes rich in glacial silt, paints its surroundings in vibrant, chalky tones of turquoise.

One of the cleanest natural environments remaining in the world, the area was not granted formal protection until 1959. At that time the Chilean government created Parque Nacional Lago de Grey, a 15-square-mile tract of land near the Paine massif that was in danger of being deforested and overgrazed by sheep and cattle. Renamed after the mountain range when it was expanded to its current size in 1962, Torres del Paine National Park has earned a reputation worldwide as the crown jewel of South American wilderness areas. In 1978 the park was classified as a World Heritage Biospheric Reserve by the United Nations.

Within the boundaries of the park, there is an extraordinary convergence of ecosystems. Below the mountain peaks lie a huge ice field and glaciers. Runoff from the melting ice feeds numerous streams, rivers and lakes. These are scattered across a forested highland plateau that gradually drops to the level of the pampas. Blessed with this varied habitat, the park is home to a rich diversity of wildlife. There are more than 40 different species of mammals alone—a surprisingly high number for a park on a continent with a scarcity of large animals.

The largest bird capable of prolonged flight, the condor soars on fully extended wings, swooping down to search for carrion.

Fading light subdues the brooding, cloud-engulfed peaks of Cuernos del Paine.

Deep within the forests along the undulating southern foothills, pumas skulk on silent, padded paws. Hiding in the shadows of gnarled lenga trees, these 150-pound cats are fierce predators. The males and females stake out overlapping home ranges as broad as 40 square miles. Although they prefer the dense cover of woodlands or the rocky flanks of mountains, where they sometimes hole up in caves, they have been known to prowl almost any type of habitat, even entering the swamps. So adaptive are pumas that they have become the wild cats known by many names: mountain lions, panthers, catamounts, cougars. Agile and elusive, pumas can travel 10 miles across rivers and rugged terrain in a few hours.

Sheep, first introduced to this part of the world in the late 1800s, have been the easy prey to the pumas. To control the population of the big cats, one or two lion hunters, or leoneros, were employed by every estancia. But with the protection afforded by the park and a 1980 Chilean law prohibiting the killing of pumas, the numbers of the cats have steadily increased.

Meadows florid with foxgloves and ox-eye daisies feed grazing herds of guanacos. Members of the camel family, guanacos are also kin to the now-domesticated llamas. Both species are descendants of a jackrabbit-size animal that originated in North America more than 40 million years ago. The guanacos evolved into the tallest mammals in South America. With their padded hooves, they are also among the most graceful, sure-footed across deep snow, rocky hills or even sinking sands. Yet their fluid movements and aristocratic elegance are not at all in keeping with some of their more vulgar habits: For one thing, their welcoming greeting is a boorish, turkey-like gobble of protest that is accompanied, often as not, by an offensive gob of half-digested grasses.

While the guanacos tend to stay together in herds, the Andean dwarf deer known as the pudú leads a relatively solitary existence. It forages in the seclusion of the dense, rain-soaked forests that line the fjords along the western periphery of the park. Thought possibly to be a distant relative of both the North American mule and the black-tailed deer, the

shy pudú more closely resembles a small antelope. Short-legged and stocky, it stands a mere 15 inches tall and weighs less than 25 pounds. Thanks to the refuge of the park, the pudú, an endangered species, is isolated from the poachers, loggers and ranchers who drove it to the brink of extinction during the last century.

The park also provides sanctuary for the diminutive gray fox. Sixteen inches high at the shoulder and from six to nine pounds when fully grown, the gray fox of Patagonia is unique to the world. Some six or seven million years ago, these animals had already

separated from the wolf-like lineage still common in North America and Europe. About a million years later, they migrated across the Isthmus of Panama into South America where they evolved further, becoming a distinct species that no longer even belonged to the genus *Vulpes*.

Omnivorous creatures, the gray foxes are partial to European hares—brought to this part of the continent in the 1880s—along with mice, frogs, lizards and rabbit-like rodents called cavies. Their diet also includes berries, small birds and eggs, and insects such as beetles. They are indiscriminate scav-

Surprised while stealing across the pampas, a Patagonian gray fox freezes in its tracks.

engers as well and will dine on the half-eaten leftovers of pumas.

While they are notably unrestrained in what they eat, gray foxes are also remarkably cooperative in obtaining food. Females without litters of their own often assist in bringing meals to families of pups. Such instincts help the gray foxes in their competition for survival with rivals such as Geoffroy's cats and the coyote-size colored foxes known as culpeos. Seldom straying very far from areas where European hares are plentiful, these other creatures are not as keen on a widely varied diet.

No other continent is endowed with a greater number of bird species than South America, and Torres del Paine National Park attracts its fair share. An estimated 435 different varieties of birds either inhabit this part of the world or fly through it on their annual migrations.

Buff-necked ibises called bandurria poke around in the reedy marshes with long, black, downward-curving bills. They raucously signal their presence with loud, metallic honks. Black-necked swans, cormorants, upland geese and ducks of the crested families swim the lakes and tarns of the foothills, while flamingos contribute a shocking touch of pink to the landscape. Flitting among stands of lenga trees are red-breasted meadow larks, Magellanic woodpeckers known locally as carpinteros negros, and parakeet-like birds called catitas or caturras. High overhead in the pewter skies, stately condors, eagles and peregrine falcons ride la escoba de Dios.

In this place where the winds scour the underbelly of the world, local lore and beliefs gain credence. According to one Patagonian legend, whoever eats a sweet, seed-filled calafate—fruit of the region's spiny, box-leafed barberry shrub—is destined to return to this land. Yet even if the berries are not in season, the mere sight of the granite towers rising behind the shrubs would be enough to fill most adventuresome visitors to the park with a strong desire to come back.

*I*N 1991 I AGREED TO BE A GUEST LECTURER ON A
cruise to Antarctica—for many years the only continent to which I had never been. Having read about the
expeditions of explorers such as Amundsen, Scott and
Shackleton, I had long yearned to experience first-hand
the polar wilderness at the bottom of the world.

We flew out of Chile to the Falkland Islands, where
we met our ship and began a three-day voyage to the
South Shetland Islands across the Drake Passage. One of
the roughest sea channels in the world, these waters are
a hostile yellowish-gray with barely a hint of blue.
Conditions for us were stormy, but tolerable. The thought
of sailing vessels from an earlier time waiting six months
for passable weather was somewhat consoling.

Trailing behind us above the wake of the ship was a
wandering albatross, a thrilling sight that fulfilled one of
my most cherished hopes for the trip. This is the world's
largest flying bird, with foot-wide wings that spread
12 feet or more. Beautifully adapted for effortless gliding,
it can travel thousands of miles, riding on the updrafts
just above the waves and seldom needing to flap its wings.

Passing Elephant Island evoked the memory of Sir
Ernest Shackleton and one of the most incredible adventure stories in the history of exploration. In 1915, his ship
crushed by ice, Shackleton left 22 men on the frozen shores
and sailed with a crew of five in an open boat nearly
800 miles across the raging Scotia Sea to South Georgia
Island. Returning to rescue the castaways, he found them
sheltering under overturned lifeboats, subsisting on penguin and seal meat. Miraculously, not one life was lost.

Welded by ice to the southernmost continent, the
Antarctic Peninsula reaches
1,200 miles north before
falling into the stormy seas
about 670 miles off the
coast of South America.

steep mountains rising sheer from the sea along both banks. Reflections of the snowy peaks in the smooth, dark waters were perfect mirror-images.

We landed several times to visit penguin rookeries, including one of Adélies that is the largest in the antarctic. Climbing to the top of a ridge, I was treated to the awesome spectacle of about a million of the tuxedoed revelers waddling about, sliding down icy slopes, and flopping into the frigid waters.

Then came my most intense feeling of remoteness. Four of us went off in a Zodiac to a bay beyond earshot of the noisy rookery. As we sat in the boat on the cold, unmoving waters surrounded by motionless icebergs and floe chunks, I was overwhelmed by the silence. I could almost hear the blood coursing through my arteries.

After a tour of Bellingshausen base on King George Island, I was granted another one of my wishes: to see a leopard seal, an antarctic predator that attacks even large, adult penguins. Our Zodiac got hung up as we left the island and the second mate got out to help push it into deeper waters. As he did, he was charged by a ferocious, quarter-ton leopard seal. He jumped right back into the boat pretty quickly! The leopard seal soon swam off, and we later learned that people at the base had been feeding it, which accounted for its extreme aggressiveness.

Although temperatures sometimes rose above freezing, the mild weather was offset by harsh, cold gusts of so-called katabatic winds. By the time upper-level air masses from warmer environments arrives at Antarctica, most of the moisture has been squeezed out. Intensely chilled, this air descends over the central polar plateau, building in velocity to as much as 180 miles per hour as it hits the coast. During one katabatic blow, the engine of our ship cut out as we passed through a vast meadow of krill; swarming in tremendous density, they were sucked up and clogged the filters, causing the engine to overheat and shut down. Tensions mounted as the ship was swept across a bay toward some threatening rocks. Fortunately, the crew managed to start the auxiliary engine and line the ship up into the wind, averting a sure disaster.

Conflicting emotions of exhilaration and terror somehow work like magnetic forces for Antarctica. "One goes there once and gets the fever and can't stop going," Shackleton wrote. His colleague, Frank Wild, talked about "the little voices" that kept summoning him back. The little voices had spoken to one man in our group who in his youth had spent six months mapping Antarctica. For 30 years the continent had been beckoning him and at last he had heeded the call to return. I hope the wait is not nearly as long for my opportunity to do likewise.

—JF

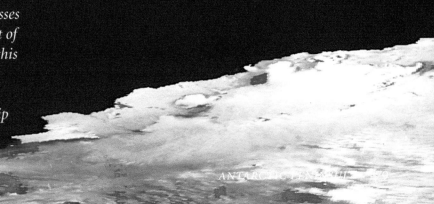

ANTARCTIC PENINSULA

BY LES LINE

Clenching the South Pole in a white-mittened fist, Antarctica appears to be pointing toward more hospitable environments to the north. The extended, frostbitten finger of the continent is the Antarctic Peninsula, a 1,200-mile-long protrusion of windswept rock and ice.

This is the bloodless extremity of a frigid place as severe as outer space. Temperatures here can dive as low as -129.6°F., rivaling sites on Mars. A permanent ice sheet nursed by snows built up over many thousands of years reflects sunlight, adding to the chill. And although the ice of the continent holds three-quarters of the world's fresh water, most of the region is desert. So freeze-locked is the moisture of the region that blizzards are more often a wind-driven redistributing of existing snow than an actual snowfall. Even in the austral summer most of the shores remain icebound, walled behind blue glaciers that, from time to time, cast off great chunks into the open waters.

Flanked by islands, the region is a frozen archipelago of chilling adventure and imperiling cold. Many features on this landscape carry the names of celebrated explorers and their discoveries: Palmer Land, recalling the sealer whose sighting of the continent in 1820 was among the very first; Erebus and Terror Gulf, named after the ships of an 1841 expedition that were first to penetrate through the pack ice; Elephant Island, so called for its gigantic seals with their trunk-like snouts.

Other landmarks bear names that sound a warning or describe the emotions the locations have evoked: Whirlwind Inlet, Danger Islands, Deception Island, Cape Longing, Cape Disappointment, Eternity Range.

Rising to 13,747 feet at Mount Jackson in Palmer Land, the ice-clad peaks that form the spine of the Antarctic Peninsula are the tail of the mighty Andes in South America. Pushing up from a curved submarine ridge that links Tierra del Fuego with the peninsula, drowning volcanoes raise their heads from stormy seas to form the islands of South Orkney, South Sandwich and South Georgia. Strictly speaking, the peninsula itself is actually an island: It is a block of bedrock isolated from land by a deep-sea trough. But the peninsula is fused to the continental mass of Antarctica by an ice cap thousands of feet thick.

The northernmost tip of the Antarctic Peninsula is the point on the continent most distant from the South Pole—roughly 1,850 miles as the skua flies. It is also the point closest to South America, which is some 670 miles away. And it is virtually the only point on its continent north of the Antarctic Circle, the imaginary line south of which the sun never shines in winter. In damp, sheltered spots along the west coast at this end of the peninsula there are clumps of mosses, lichens and hair grasses—one of the two vascular plants that grow in Antarctica. Here also is found the continent's largest terrestrial ani-

Beaches of black ash betray the volcanic origin of Deception Island, a still-active caldera.

Propped up on a cold, hard bed, a restless elephant seal scratches its chest before settling down to sleep with others of its colony.

mal: a wingless midge that measures less than a quarter of an inch in length.

This was not always the case. According to the latest theories of continental drift, Antarctica was at one time united with South America, Africa, India and Australia in a supercontinent that geologists have named Gondwana. In that long-ago era, a host of land-dwelling animals—most of them likely to remain forever unknown—resided in Antarctica's forests, at home among flourishing stands of conifers, sequoias, beeches and fig trees. Since 1902 a steep bluff of Seymour Island off the Antarctic Peninsula has yielded a succession of fossil treasures, not only of plants and trees but also of animals. Among the species memorialized in the fossils are a small fruit-eating marsupial, a tall flightless bird, an armadillo and a crocodile. Also found were the teeth and jawbones of an animal that is believed to have been the size of a small horse and to have closely resembled the guanaco, a present-day Andean species related to the llama and the camel. This first ever record of a large, herbivorous mammal having lived on the southernmost continent, the discovery is touted as further proof that Antarctica and South America shared the same community of wildlife as recently as 40 million years ago.

But the separation of the continents—Australia is thought to have been the last to split—eventually left Antarctica adrift, encircled by frigid waters. Ice conquered the con-

Adélie penguins line up at a rocky shore, politely waiting their turn to leap into the frigid waters.

Wings useless for flying propel an underwater emperor penguin at up to 30 miles an hour.

tinent some 25 million years ago, crushing the forests under sheets as much as 15,700 feet thick. Today no more than five percent of the coastline is ice-free, most of it along the western shores of the Antarctic Peninsula.

Who first discovered this wilderness of unyielding cold? England, Russia and the United States have all claimed the formal honor. English Captain James Cook sailed his ship the *Resolution* across the Antarctic Circle three times between 1772 and 1775. He came within a hundred miles of the continent before being thwarted by impenetrable ice. In 1820 another Englishman, Edward Bransfield, charted the shores of what he called Trinity Land. But American officials would later contend that what he had seen was only an island and not the mainland itself. Fabian von Bellingshausen, a Russian admiral and scientist, circumnavigated the continent early in 1821. But the land that he named Alexander I for his czar turned out to be a huge island, separated from the base of the peninsula by an icebound sound. Three

OVERLEAF: *Dusk silhouettes a flotilla of icebergs off the bleak Argentine Islands.*

BELOW: *Requiring more than two months to incubate eggs, giant petrels must breed early in the spring to rear their slow-growing chicks before winter.*

months earlier, Nathaniel Brown Palmer of the United States had sighted the Antarctic Peninsula from his ship *Hero* while searching for seal rookeries. For a short time the place was even called Palmer Peninsula, in tribute to what was considered a rather unimportant discovery.

An aloof, brutal region that has never been home to an indigenous human population, the continent at first went largely ignored except by sealers such as Palmer. Within five decades of Cook's early reports of fur seals along the shores of the subantarctic islands, the population was decimated and new colonies were being sought.

Seals beyond counting were found on the antarctic ice, but none with the luxurious pelage of the fur seal.

The so-called true seals found by the hunters differed from the sought-after fur seals in a number of important ways. One difference was their mobility on land. The true seals barely managed to hump along with their clawed fore flippers. The fur seals, by contrast, were relatively agile, having mastered the use of all four limbs. Another difference was what disappointed the hunters. The fur seals had an inner layer of thick, soft hair as insulation against the cold. The true seals relied on blubber to keep them warm.

When no new colonies of fur seals could be found in the 1820s, frustrated sealers turned for a time to hunting the elephant seals. They raided the rookeries of four-ton bulls and rendered the blubber into oil. Thankfully, though, the elephant seal never inspired the type of systematic harvesting that brought the fur seal to the brink of extinction.

Like the fur seals, the elephant seals breed on widely separated groups of islands well north of the Antarctic Circle. There are also colonies on islands off the tip of the Antarctic Peninsula, where dominant males called beachmasters defend harems of perhaps two dozen cows, the females only about a quarter their size. Fattened on a diet of fish, squid and octopus before they haul ashore to claim their territories, the beachmasters fast for three months while they scar up their bodies, chasing off would-be rivals. Resonating through inflated trunks, the strident roars of the warring bulls can seem enough to crack the ice far to the south.

The four families of seals that dwell on the antarctic ice never set flipper on land. Smallest are the Ross seals, solitary creatures rarely seen. Their large, imploring eyes plead innocence, but little is known of their habits.

Weddell seals, however, are among the most familiar of marine mammals. They are

named after British navigator James Weddell, who explored the region in 1823. The seals spend much of the time beneath the fast ice near the coast, especially during the dark winter. They surface every hour or so to the breathing holes that they cut with their teeth. In the murky darkness beneath the ice, they rely on their built-in sonar to detect fish and squid, diving effortlessly to depths of more than 1,500 feet to fetch this food. In the spring, the cows assemble on top of the ice to pup while the dominant males maintain their guard of the mating labyrinths in the

frigid waters below. Except for the sled dogs of polar explorers, no other mammals have ventured so far south. One breeding colony was found nearly 300 miles inside the Ross Ice Shelf where rifts had provided access to the waters under the thick ice.

Tens of millions of crabeater seals—the world's most plentiful species of marine mammal—live out their entire 40-year lives on the pack ice. Filtering krill through teeth that function like the baleen of a whale, they dart through the iceberg-choked waters, maneuvering their sleek, cream-colored forms in porpoise-like ballets.

Haunting the ice floes are leopard seals, spotted like their namesake and every bit as ferocious. Ten feet long and weighing about 700 pounds, these powerful carnivores can literally shake a penguin out of its skin before swallowing it whole. Formidable predators, they have an astounding ability to torpedo out of the waters onto ice platforms as much as eight feet high.

But if the leopard seal is the predatory terror of antarctic waters, the skua is the eagle of antarctic skies. This gull-like raptor is equipped with talons on its webbed feet and touts a wickedly hooked bill that can gouge out the eyes of a newborn seal in one swooping moment. Three pounds of feathered malevolence, the mighty skua can fell an inattentive human intruder with a single claw-raking blow to the head. This hunter's plundering of eggs, hatchlings and even full-

Presenting less than a fifth of their bulk above the water, giant icebergs set loose by the frozen cliffs on shore reflect the setting sun.

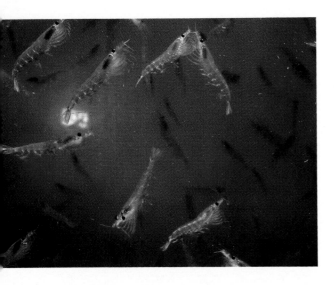

Krill grow as they feed on the plentiful phytoplankton in summer, then shrink as they consume the energy of their own bodies to survive winter.

grown fledglings affects the many species of seabirds that nest in the region: imperial shags, kelp gulls, prions, antarctic terns, storm petrels, snow petrels, fulmars, sheathbills, penguins. Not even the vomit-spewing self-defense of the giant petrel chicks is a sufficient deterrent.

Screaming imperially from the sky, the ruthless skuas divide the breeding colonies of Adélie penguins into territorial killing grounds. In a single nesting season, 181 pairs of ruling skuas once took an estimated 2,000 eggs and 10,000 chicks out of a rookery of 60,000 nests. But while they may seem to exact a fearsome toll, they actually prevent an even worse carnage by fending off other interloping skuas that would challenge them for their domains; the territorial battles are sometimes to the death. As well, about half of the eggs that the skuas steal are infertile or cold-damaged, and many of the chicks they take would perish by other means.

The prolific coastal fringe of Antarctica is nurtured by the sea. Encircling the continent about 1,000 miles offshore is a natural barrier where cold, fresh polar waters collide with the warmer salt waters of the Atlantic,

Pacific and Indian Oceans. The Antarctic Convergence as this ocean region is called marks the frontier of the realm of the krill—semi-transparent crustaceans as much as two-and-a-half inches long that directly or indirectly support almost all other antarctic wildlife. A key link in one of the world's shortest food chains, krill feed on one-celled sea plants called phytoplankton and nourish the region's many communities of fish, seals, winged seabirds, penguins and whales. The population explosion of the krill during the austral summer turns the waters into a reddish-tinged broth.

The gentoo, chinstrap and macaroni penguins of the Antarctic Peninsula and its

Spewing water filtered of food in its baleen, a humpback steams across an ice-littered bay.

700 million tons, or roughly ten times the annual seafood harvest by humans worldwide. This bounty of crustacean life has endowed the region with thriving communities of whales. The blue whales, largest of the baleen family, consume about three tons of krill apiece every day. The minke whales, smaller but most numerous, are also krill eaters. Deep-diving sperm whales feast on tons of krill-fed squid.

During the 1890s, some 60 years after the sealers had abandoned the region, whalers arrived and began to annihilate the great cetaceans. By the 1930s the austral-summer kill topped 40,000, with blue and humpback whales suffering the heaviest losses. Then, the whalers turned to sperm and fin whales, which were likewise reduced. By the time that commercial whaling was effectively restricted in the mid-1980s, the extinction of several species was near at hand. About 1,000 blue whales survive where once there were 200,000. The humpbacks number only three percent of their former abundance.

Today supertrawlers with onboard processing plants catch, freeze and can krill for human consumption. And with the increase in commercial harvesting of the region's life-giving resource, there is seemingly justifiable concern about the effect on the entire antarctic ecosystem. As naturalist Louis J. Halle has pointed out, for the wildlife of the area "krill is the staff of life—more so than bread ever was for any human community."

offshore islands are not particularly light eaters, but the krill requirements of the huge colonies of Adélie penguins are genuinely mind-boggling. At the beginning of the nesting season, the birds parade in pairs across some 60 miles of pack ice to their shoreline rookeries. Among rocks that the wind has swept free of snow, the females lay two eggs on average, then alternate with their mates between incubation duties and week-long feeding excursions. By the peak of the nesting season, the Adélie colony is consuming 2,000 tons of krill each day.

The krill, however, are truly abundant, probably numbering in the trillions. Their biomass has been estimated at as much as

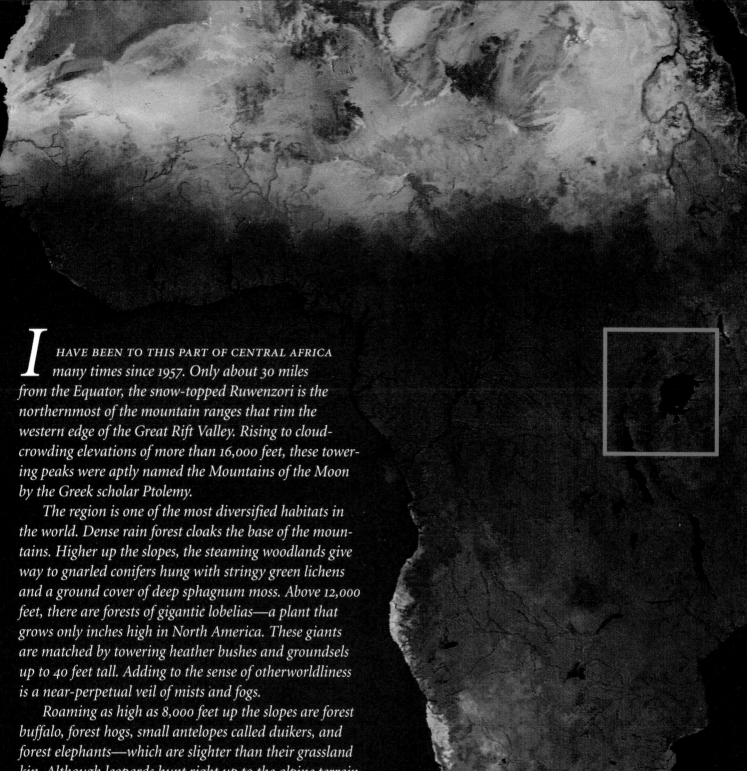

I HAVE BEEN TO THIS PART OF CENTRAL AFRICA
*many times since 1957. Only about 30 miles
from the Equator, the snow-topped Ruwenzori is the
northernmost of the mountain ranges that rim the
western edge of the Great Rift Valley. Rising to cloud-
crowding elevations of more than 16,000 feet, these towering peaks were aptly named the Mountains of the Moon
by the Greek scholar Ptolemy.*

*The region is one of the most diversified habitats in
the world. Dense rain forest cloaks the base of the mountains. Higher up the slopes, the steaming woodlands give
way to gnarled conifers hung with stringy green lichens
and a ground cover of deep sphagnum moss. Above 12,000
feet, there are forests of gigantic lobelias—a plant that
grows only inches high in North America. These giants
are matched by towering heather bushes and groundsels
up to 40 feet tall. Adding to the sense of otherworldliness
is a near-perpetual veil of mists and fogs.*

*Roaming as high as 8,000 feet up the slopes are forest
buffalo, forest hogs, small antelopes called duikers, and
forest elephants—which are slighter than their grassland
kin. Although leopards hunt right up to the alpine terrain,
our guides were always much more afraid of the buffalo.
These burly beasts pack as much as 1,500 pounds into a
nearly hairless hide well suited to hot weather. When
threatened, they can charge at full speed through brush so
thick that even a fright-spurred human could barely
crawl into it for cover.*

*On the lower slopes of the Ruwenzori there are
crowned eagles, beautifully crested and with wingspans of
up to six feet. I had the good fortune to come across the
first of their nests ever to be discovered. On another day, a
photographer and I followed a group of young colobus*

Known as the Mountains of the Moon,
the snowcapped, cloud-shrouded Ruwenzori
range spans a distance of about 75 miles along
the border between Zaire and Uganda.

monkeys in hopes of getting pictures as they were hunted by a crowned eagle. Tracing an established route of the monkeys through the forest canopy, we found a gap in their aerial highway where they would leap across open sky from one tree to the next. While we waited quietly, there was a sudden commotion as several monkeys tumbled to the forest floor. I looked up and spied a male crowned eagle circling overhead, but it struck me as being far too high to provoke the keen agitation of the monkeys. Then, a female crowned eagle suddenly swooped down right before us, almost snatching one of the monkeys as they scattered to hide. The male had been acting as a decoy, which surprised me because I had never before seen crowned eagles hunt in pairs.

Farther south, the Virunga Volcanoes along the border between Zaire and Rwanda are the last stronghold of the endangered mountain gorilla. On my first encounter with a family of these creatures, I was sitting on the ground in a grove of bamboo when two curious juveniles came down from their perches to examine me. They even touched my hair. The trick to avoiding a clash with the silverback—the dominant male of a family—is to refrain from any kind of action that might be interpreted as competition. There are a few basic rules: Crouch as low to the ground as possible; never move between the females and the silverback; and never look the silverback in the eye. If a silverback charges, the drill is to stay quiet, act submissively and keep looking down.

On a trip to the Rwanda side of the Virungas in 1987, a photographer and I witnessed a confrontation between two silverbacks near the Karisoke Research Centre established by Dian Fossey. The silverback of one family was about 50 feet from us, while the challenging silverback of another family was almost half a mile away across the valley. Although we could hardly see him through the forest, we could hear him roar and slap his chest. He shook bushes, tore the limbs off trees and beat down the grass in a rampage. As we watched, the silverback near us set off to perform a similar spectacle. He looked back in our direction, then beat his chest and shook some bushes. We thought he was bluffing—until he started charging toward us. On the way, he reached up and snapped a limb about five inches in diameter off a tree. As the photographer leapt under a log, I stuck my head in some bushes that were thick with nettles. The silverback stormed right up between us. Out of the corner of my eye I could see one of his big, hairy feet planted about three feet away from me. I resisted the urge to look up and see what he intended to do with the limb he was swinging. Within about half a minute—which seemed an eternity—the silverback decided that we no longer posed a threat. He calmly wandered off, eating bamboo shoots and wild celery as though nothing had happened. We were not quite so quick to regain our composure.

The mountain gorillas convey most powerfully the feeling of wildness in this part of Africa. Perhaps because they represent an early stage in the evolutionary path of humans, the very sight of one of them evokes an immediate bond—a link to something incredibly ancient. And in order for the mountain gorillas to survive, at least a part of their habitat must be kept intact; a part of the earth must be forever wild.

—JF

MOUNTAINS OF THE MOON

BY BOYD NORTON

Swirling mist softens and diffuses the dawn light. On every leaf and branch, beads of moisture collect and coalesce, intensifying the sense of lush verdancy that permeates rain forest. The morning air is deeply chilled, a seeming paradox in a land barely 100 miles south of the Equator. But altitude, not latitude, dictates climate here; these slopes climb to elevations of more than 9,000 feet and, in places, reach beyond 11,000 feet.

This is a world gone mad with green, every hue and tone imaginable. Stinging nettles over six feet high battle for space with legions of ferns and vines. Towering above are hypericum trees, their branches tipped with bright yellow, rose-like blooms. Tall, spindly bamboo is packed so densely that no human can squeeze through. Elsewhere, gnarled hagenia trees reach skyward, their outstretched limbs draped in lichens and mosses. As if lifted from the pages of Tolkien or Grimm, the landscape is at once mysterious, foreboding and enchanting.

Within the greenery, a dark, hulking form stirs. A massive head, cloaked in fur that is black but tinged with silvery gray, rises suddenly out of a tangle of ferns. Soft, brown eyes in an almost-human face blink sleepily. Then, a hand emerges, plucks a green morsel from a vine, and daintily delivers it to a yawning mouth.

Dawn is the time for families of mountain gorillas to rouse themselves and begin feeding. The big silverback, leader of this clan, sits munching as his eyelids droop, alternately dozing and chewing. Soon the other family members, the females, younger males, and youngsters—about a dozen in all—abandon their night's nests to sample the leaves and stems of favored foliage. The nests were built the previous evening by bending down vegetation to form soft mattresses on the otherwise hard, damp ground. New ones will be crafted later on, wherever nightfall finds the family.

Finally, the silverback, having overcome his drowsiness, stumbles from his nest, walking knuckles-and-feet on all fours in a slow, ambling gait. As the clan drifts through the forest, a shaft of light pierces the mist and foliage, offering hope that perhaps part of the day will be sunny and warm.

The luxuriant home of the great apes sits on the flank of one of several ancient volcanoes that split the borders separating Zaire, Rwanda and Uganda. The high-altitude rain forest blanketing the slopes of these Virunga Volcanoes forms the habitat for the last remaining clans of mountain gorillas. *Gorilla gorilla beringei* was not identified as a species distinct from the more numerous lowland gorilla of the Congo (Zaire) Basin until 1902. By then, most other wildlife had long since been cataloged. Biologists believe there are no more than about 600 of these animals left in the wild, half of them in two adjoining reserves: Virunga National Park in Zaire and Volcanoes National Park in Rwanda.

Flowering red hot pokers thrust skyward before the distant Mount Gahinga.

When the continent was called darkest Africa, this was its heart, a vast region made impenetrable by dense, malarial forests and daunting mountains. Many early adventurers disappeared without a trace. Long after the savannahs of East Africa, this region was the last to be explored. Parts of it did not yield their secrets until well into this century.

Two British explorers, John Hanning Speke and Sir Richard Burton, discovered Lake Tanganyika in 1858 after an overland trek from the coast of present-day Tanzania. In 1861 Speke returned, setting forth from Zanzibar on an arduous trip that would take him to the shores of Lake Victoria in his quest for the source of the Nile. As he stood on a rise of land near the border of Tanzania, Speke noted "some bold sky-scraping cones situated in the country of Ruanda" to the west of where he stood. This *terra incognita* was the southern extremity of the Mountains of the Moon. Speke called them by their native name, Mfumbiro, in his journal. "The Mfumbiro cones in Ruanda, which I believe reach 10,000 feet, are said to be the highest of the 'Mountains of the Moon.'" In obvious reference to the mountain gorillas, he reported that natives had told him "there were monsters who could not converse with men, and never showed themselves unless they saw women pass by; then, in voluptuous excitement, they squeezed them to death." It was but one of many slanderous tales about the gentle creatures.

The Virunga Volcanoes form part of Africa's fiery spine, a crescent-shaped range of mountains—called Mitumba—that mark the western limit of the Great Rift Valley. This arc of rugged peaks runs northward from Lake Tanganyika, skirts Lake Kivu and Lake Edward, rises like a rampart above the game-filled Ruindi and Rutshuru Plains, and reaches its culmination at more than 16,000 feet in the breathtaking Ruwenzori massif. These are the Mountains of the Moon, for so they were described in A.D. 150 by the mathematician and geographer Ptolemy. From North African legends of a great mountain range in the mysterious interior, he deduced that the *Lunae Montes* were the source of the Nile. Seventeen centuries later he would be proven correct, or nearly so. Waters plunging from the slopes of the Virunga Volcanoes and the Ruwenzori eventually reach Lake Victoria, the Nile's true source.

Thick-trunked groundsels and slender-stemmed lobelias sport a leafy regalia befitting their extraordinary stature.

As its eyes detect changes in the light, a chameleon adjusts its color camouflage.

The Ruwenzori, loftiest of the *Lunae Montes*, were not revealed to Western explorers for almost three more decades. Henry Morton Stanley, an American journalist with a strong appetite for adventure, skirted the area in 1866 in search of the missionary David Livingstone. (He uttered his famous "Dr. Livingstone, I presume?" at Ujiji on the northeast shore of Lake Tanganyika.) Having sampled the savage splendor of the region, Stanley returned for more intensive explorations of central Africa. While camped on the shore of Lake Albert in 1888, he was astonished one day to find a spectacular snow-clad mountain range that had been shrouded by clouds for weeks. Stanley put their elevation at 15,000 feet and learned that in the local Olukonjo language they were called Ru-Nsoro, meaning "snow" or "snowy mountains." (In later translations, the name is interpreted as "rainmaker.")

That the peaks had eluded discovery for so long is not altogether surprising. With nine summits over 16,000 feet—one of them, Mount Margherita, reaches 16,763 feet—the Ruwenzori massif generates its own climate, and most of the weather is bad. For an average of 300 days each year, the mountains are lost in a cover of thick, dark clouds.

The entire chain of mountains from the Ruwenzori to the Virungas is of keen interest to biologists, botanists and zoologists. On the

Overdressed hagenia trees stretch limbs wrapped in boas of lichens, vines and mosses.

ABOVE: *With soothing gentleness, a mountain gorilla grooms a family member.* RIGHT, ABOVE: *Coddled by his mother, a young ape samples the foliage.* RIGHT: *A yawning silverback bares his teeth.*

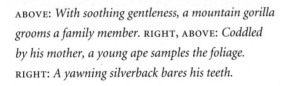

A family of mountain gorillas ambles through the dense forest growth of Virunga National Park.

OVERLEAF: *Curtains of cloud lift off the slopes of Mount Visoke in Parc National des Volcans, unveiling the lofty upper reaches of Mount Karisimbe (left) and Mount Mikeno (right).*

slopes of the Ruwenzori are found some of the world's most unusual plants and animals. At the lowest elevations, grasses six feet in height offer a partial cover to the ten-foot-tall elephants that feed on them. Higher up, at 7,000 feet, in a lush zone of evergreens, there are earthworms more than three feet long and triple-horned chameleons. Amid wild bananas and tree ferns, sunbirds flit from flower to flower, sipping nectar like hummingbirds. Higher still, on the slopes above 7,500 feet, bamboo flourishes and leopards roam in search of prey such as duikers, monkeys and rock hyraxes—rabbit-sized animals that are the closest relative to the elephant. On the moorlands above the forests, at about 11,000 feet, there are gigantic versions of common plants such as lobelias, heathers and groundsels.

Among those drawn to the Mountains of the Moon was American naturalist Carl Akeley. Fascinated by the discovery of the mountain gorilla, he led an expedition to the Virunga Volcanoes in 1921. Already there were signs that the species was in danger: Adventurers were coming from around the world to hunt the gorillas as trophies. The territory had become part of the vast Belgian Congo and Akeley mounted a successful campaign for preservation. In 1925 King Albert of Belgium created by royal decree the 60,000 acre Parc National Albert, protecting the heart of the Virunga Volcanoes. On Akeley's return to the region in 1926, he contracted a mysterious ailment and died. He was buried in the forest of the Virungas, a site he had deemed "the most beautiful spot in all the world."

Through the dedicated efforts of the naturalist's widow, Mary Jobe Akeley, Parc National Albert was expanded in 1929 to enclose more than 500,000 acres—a nearly

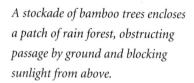

LEFT: *When the hyrax senses danger, an unusual patch of hair on its back blooms like a flower.* BELOW: *A female bushbuck stands watch over an area where the young of the herd have been hidden.*

A stockade of bamboo trees encloses a patch of rain forest, obstructing passage by ground and blocking sunlight from above.

ten-fold increase in area. Renamed Virunga National Park after Zaire had gained independence, it extended northward to take in the Ruwenzori, as well as the Ruindi and Rutshuru Plains between the Virungas and the Ruwenzori. Further protection came in 1952 with the creation of Queen Elizabeth National Park (now Ruwenzori National Park) in western Uganda. When Rwanda became an independent nation in 1962, the portion of Parc National Albert along its side of the Virungas became Parc National des Volcans (Volcanoes National Park).

A journey southward from the slopes of Ruwenzori makes obvious that Virunga has the most varied habitat anywhere in Africa. From snow to treeless tundra, past moors and rain forest, the land abruptly turns flat and dry, much like the savannahs of Kenya and Tanzania. In the Ruindi grasses there are herds of kob, graceful antelopes that resemble impala. The herbivore tribes include buffalo, waterbuck and topi. In Swahili, the topi is called Mnyama wa rangi tano, or "the beast of five colors," for its variegated tones, which range from mahogany to purplish red and iridescent, gun-metal blue. Almost every watering place, from river to lake to mudhole, is a home to hippopotamuses. For some unknown reason, this region has the highest density of the animals anywhere in Africa. There are also large herds of big-tusked elephants, although the population on the Uganda side is only now beginning to recover from the slaughter that occurred during the country's civil war in the 1970s.

Where there are game herds, there are carnivores. One of the rarest is the wild, or hunting, dog. Called "painted wolves" for their mottled yellow-black-brown splotches, the wild dogs hunt in packs like wolves. Following their dominant male, they trot along at the fringe of a game herd, darting in and out as they scout for animals too weak or infirm to escape them. When their quarry has been chosen, they work cooperatively. Two or more will chase the targeted victim while the others circle in from another direction. They close in quickly, teeth slashing, to gorge themselves before hyenas or lions can usurp their kill.

ABOVE, TOP: *Helichrysum bloom like burst ground-cover buttons.* BOTTOM: *A purple-breasted sunbird siphons nectar from a lobelia.*

Lions roaming these grasslands take advantage of their tawny coloring to conceal themselves while they await an unwary topi, buffalo or kob. The females of a pride do most of the hunting, sometimes working as a team like the wild dogs. But the lions lack the speed of the canines, and must rely on stealth, strength and numbers to bring down prey, their powerful jaws clamping over the nose or throat to suffocate. The dominant male, never far off, rushes in to claim his share of the kill, and only after he has eaten

*A ground-roosting species of lobelia sprouts a
cabbage-like rosette 18 inches in diameter.*

do the others dare to feast. A large kill, such as a buffalo, may sate a pride for days.

Leopards prowl the bordering forests, venturing onto the grasslands at night to hunt. These powerful cats often haul their downed victims—sometimes antelopes that outweigh them—up into trees to escape marauding hyenas and lions. Safely off the ground, they can dine at their leisure, then sleep by day draped over branches.

Farther south the Ruindi and Rutshuru Plains wrinkle into hills at the feet of the Virungas. Cool, green forest takes the place of the hot, dusty grasslands. In the course of a morning, the gorilla family has traveled but a few hundred yards from their night's nests. At midday, they stop for a siesta. The clouds and mist have lifted, baring a rare, blue canopy of sky. Like sunbathers at the shore, the clan sprawls in a clearing, soaking up welcome warmth. While the adults doze, the youngsters chase one another in mock battle, pounding their chests to produce "pok-pok-pok" sounds—a copy of the posturing done by the silverback to warn off intruders.

With or without sunshine, the siesta is a time of socializing for the gorillas. The young and the adults lie close together, reaching out to stroke one another's fur. Often the big silverback—some weigh nearly 400 pounds—will tenderly take up a small infant and delicately groom its coat. The mother may loll nearby, watching without concern as the silverback meticulously parts hairs, picking

out tiny parasites and bits of dirt or bark. An energetic juvenile may climb a spindly stalk of bamboo to reach the tasty, fresh leaves at the top. Not uncommonly, the bamboo will bend from the weight and the ape will come crashing down, protected by its thick fur and the cushion of the undergrowth.

Usually the sunshine is brief and swirling clouds will soon hover overhead. With a few vocalizations, the family then drifts off to find thicker vegetation. As they spread out through the tall foliage, they call to one another with a low, soft "mahem," a grunt of reassurance and contentment.

At times the peaceful routine is interrupted by confrontation. Since the home ranges of gorillas overlap, one clan inevitably meets up with another. Then, the silverbacks may engage in their "hootseries"—rounds of low-pitched "hoo-hoo-hoo" that build to an ear-splitting "wraagh!" and great shows of

chest-beating. A displaying silverback may charge into the brush, tearing up and tossing vegetation. Usually, one of the silverbacks will triumph in this game of intimidation and the other clan will move on. Sometimes matters lead to a violent clash over breeding-age females. In these instances, the antics are prelude to a charge. With their large canine teeth, the silverbacks can seriously injure each other—even cause death.

But fatal encounters are rare, and today the family wanders in peace. By late afternoon the clouds have coalesced into dark, moisture-laden vapors. Though insulated by their fur, the gorillas may huddle under a hagenia tree to escape the downpour. At dusk the rain stops and the sky brightens into the orange glow of sunset. In silence, the clan once again builds nests and curls into them to sleep.

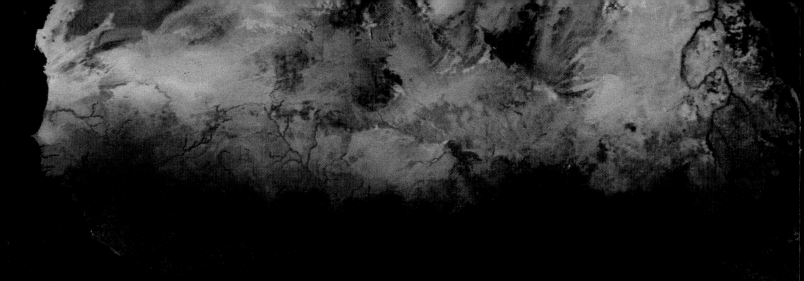

I WAS INTRODUCED TO THIS RICH OASIS IN NORTHERN
Botswana on my first trip to Africa in 1957. What
an incredible experience it was to drive for hours
through grassy savannas and forests of acacia and
mopane trees, only to arrive suddenly at the edge of the
vast expanse of marshy wetlands that is the Okavango
Delta. I remember saying to myself, "This is the real
Africa, the wild Africa I have wanted to see all my life."

I have had occasion to return to this region many
times since then, always to be impressed that it has stayed
so wild. Northern Botswana is still largely unsettled; there
are only a few small towns along with scattered camps
and lodges. And poling a mokoro into the watery maze of
shifting, reedy channels of the delta is still one of the best
ways in the world to get lost, to disappear without a trace.

This is one of the last great sanctuaries left for African
wildlife. It is home to a bewildering diversity of species:
hippopotamus, buffalo, zebra, wildebeest—even an antelope called the sitatunga that splays its hooves to walk
across floating beds of papyrus without sinking through
them. Some 400 different types of birds have been recorded in the region, including egrets, vultures, ibis, fish
eagles, herons and four-foot-tall saddle-billed storks.

There are also plenty of crocodiles, which adds a special type of excitement to water sports. On my way to the
delta once from the northeast, I was invited to go water-
skiing on the Chobe River. As I gripped the towline and
the boat started off, I saw crocodiles slip off their sandbars
into the water. I knew that if I fell there would be a race to
see who could reach me first: my companions on the boat
or the crocodiles. I made sure that I stayed up.

The region also supports what is possibly Africa's
largest remaining number of free-ranging elephants. On
one expedition with a film crew, we camped near a herd

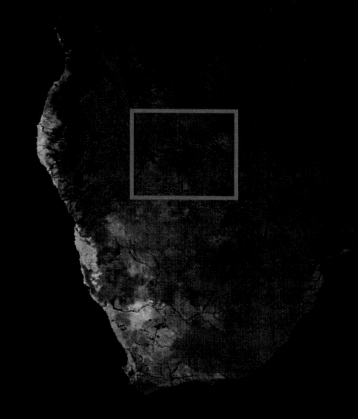

The Okavango Delta fans out over
an area of about 6,000 square miles
in northern Botswana.

east of the delta. To demonstrate an interesting behavior of elephants, I wanted to show how a charging male could be bluffed with nothing more than nerve.

With our cameraman well behind us, Simon, an elephant-wise friend and warden, and I crept up to the herd by squatting on the ground and dragging ourselves forward—what we called "bumming." The elephants were preoccupied with digging a sip well. As they pushed deep into the wet sand with their trunks, we scooted toward them. When they looked up, we froze. When they went back to work, we continued bumming closer to them. Because we kept a low profile, they probably thought we were warthogs.

When we were about 40 yards from the elephants, a bull charged us. We held our ground and waited. Puzzled that we did not run, the bull hesitated, then began to scream and kick sand at us. At just the right moment, I threw a stick at him and he backed off.

By taking advantage of the bull's indecision, I had made myself dominant. Had we yielded or attempted to flee, we could have been killed. My psychological dare, however, would not have halted a cow. I would never try to bluff a female elephant.

As the bull went off to some acacias and hid his head in the leaves, I made the mistake of turning to our cameraman to see if he had managed to film all the action. The bull saw me move and stormed back at us. Luckily, I was able to bluff him twice.

We then decided to do a good deed for the herd. Buffalo had been trying to drink at the sip wells, and the elephants had gored to death several cows—which was highly unusual. Once the herd had moved from the site, we went in with shovels to dig some new wells. Suddenly, two young bulls turned and started running straight at us, apparently thinking we were buffalo taking their water. A short distance away, the wife of our photographer was taking pictures. Fortunately, she froze. As Simon and I rushed over, waving our hats and yelling, the baffled elephants retreated. But with all the commotion, the rest of the herd had been alerted. Some 200 elephants, led by an angry cow, were now bearing down on us.

Overconfident from our earlier success in bluffing a charging bull, we had strayed much farther than we should have from our Land Rover. In the haste to reach it, our African scout ran literally out of one shoe and his pants, and we left behind a $40,000 camera. Seeing the others scramble into the cab was like watching a Marx Brothers' movie at high speed. I opted for the roof, which I could beat on to make noise. The cow pursued us for half a mile, twice just missing me with her trunk. Shaken and somewhat chastened, I was nonetheless thankful there would be no film record of the great elephant bluffer held hostage on top of a moving Land Rover by a bullying cow!

Protecting this region's wilderness is a concern now that pesticides have all but eliminated a natural safeguard: the tsetse fly. This carrier of sleeping sickness is capable of killing humans and cattle, but has no effect on wildlife. (Crediting the insect with having kept the delta wild, one warden told me that when he retired he would build a monument to it.) The coming pressures of settlements and ranching that encroach on the delta will need to be counterbalanced by an enlightened tourism industry that is committed to sustaining the local wildlife. At stake is the last, best corner of wild Africa.

—JF

OKAVANGO DELTA

BY GEORGE HARRISON

A Nile crocodile about 15 feet long lies motionless in the water one or two yards from the riverbank, waiting. Its two bulbous eyes fix on a small herd of red lechwe antelope that lingers by the shore, gleaning the shoots of sweet grasses nursed by the river's floodwaters.

A week-old lechwe kid, newest member of the herd, gambols behind its mother, pausing here and there to nip at a sprout.

Whoosh! Like a whale breaching in the ocean, the crocodile lunges from the water, its mouth agape. The startled kid is snatched and pulled into the water, vanishing with the crocodile beneath the surface. The river boils momentarily, then settles and proceeds on its slow journey. Another link in the food chain is closed.

This is the way of the Okavango Delta—life is rich, but also uncertain. Formed by the Okavango River, the delta constitutes the largest and most pristine oasis in the world, and it encompasses a magnificent natural wildlife preserve.

The Okavango is unlike any other river. While most rivers flow to a sea, this one is swallowed whole by the parched sands of the Kalahari Desert.

Born a trickle in the highlands of Angola, the Okavango River rushes southeast across Namibia's Caprivi Strip and empties into Botswana. There, it spills from a 60-mile-long pan onto a huge alluvial fan that is the world's largest inland delta. This network of interconnecting channels and waterways, choked with vast beds of reeds, papyrus and water lilies, pours six billion gallons of fresh water each day into the desert. Astronaut Wally Schirra found this 6,000-square-mile green jewel so compelling from space that he had to visit to satisfy his curiosity.

Yet, almost all of the annual 350 billion cubic feet of water evaporates as the spent Okavango dissipates into a million fingers and moves slowly, ever so slowly, to the southeast, where it vanishes altogether.

Though it now falls victim to the desert, the Okavango was once a major link in a commanding chain of rivers and swamps that carried water all the way to the Indian Ocean. The volcanic upheaval that wrought the Great Rift Valley altered this flow. Even today the river's course is constantly revised by seismic shifts in the earth's crust. Like the animals that throng the delta, the river is unpredictable, moody and ever-changing.

But water is the key that unlocks the many secrets of this wilderness wonderland. Nature usually bestows on the fortunate Okavango not one, but two wet seasons: one produced by rains between December and February, and a second one brought about by geology as the river overflows its banks between May and September. With exquisite timing, the river flooding coincides with dry weather because the rainy-season waters leaving from Angola take about six months to reach the delta.

Giraffes gather on the dry grasslands of Chobe National Park, northeast of the delta along the Savute Channel.

In futile quest of a sea, the mighty Okavango River drains into the world's largest inland delta, a sweeping alluvial oasis that disperses the waters through contorted channels into the open sands of the Kalahari Desert.

Dense beds of tassel-topped papyrus grow quickly, forever rerouting the flow of waters through the delta.

With the rising waters of summer, a water lily awakens in bloom from its silt-sheeted winter bed.

An ill-tempered hippopotamus wallows in a channel as if annoyed to be sharing the cooling waters on a hot day.

This unusual combination of wet-wet and wet-dry seasons is a luxury to which virtually all of the wildlife have become deeply attuned. With the arrival of the floods, herds of elephants, buffalo, antelope and zebra migrate north and south, their predators— lions, cheetahs, leopards, hyenas, jackals, wild dogs, vultures—trailing closely behind. Taking to the marshes for refuge are the crocodiles and the hippopotamuses, along with many different species of birds. Hundreds of other families of mammals, reptiles, amphib-

ians, insects and fish also find a bountiful existence in the wetlands.

The northeast corner of the delta holds Moremi Wildlife Reserve, 1,160 square miles of floodplain, forest, grassland, island and swamp. It is the most diversified park in Botswana. The floodplains sustain numerous species of antelope—including the reedbuck, waterbuck, lechwe, tsessebe, sable and roan—and are also the habitat for hippopotamuses, crocodiles, otters and ostriches. In the forests and on the grasslands, there

Alert for careless prey, a crocodile lurks by the shore.

A bored-looking African bull-frog squats in the shallows.

is abundant food and cover for elephants, kudus, giraffes, impalas, Cape buffaloes and zebras—as well as for the lions, leopards, wild dogs, honey badgers, and brown and spotted hyenas that are their omnipresent enemies. And nowhere on the continent is the landscape more richly endowed with as many varieties of birds.

Farther to the northeast of the delta, Chobe National Park sprawls over 30,300 square miles. Renowned for its big-game animals, the park boasts some 30,000 elephants,

which are among the noisiest on the continent. The Savute Channel that links Chobe with the Okavango River is a raucous water hole during the dry-weather season. Roaring lions and screaming spotted hyenas compete through the night for their share of a downed Cape buffalo, antelope or zebra. By day saddle-billed storks, black egrets and wattled cranes, each with their own peculiar feeding manners, hold sway among the funereal tangle of drowned tree trunks.

But the delta itself is the centerpiece of this lush wilderness table. Meandering quietly along secretive channels, a mokoro, or dugout canoe, poled by a Mbukushu native presses through thick, redolent beds of tall reeds, lilies and sedges, and passes ruddy islands of sand built by termites. The sides of the mokoro ride only inches above the water, almost at eye level to a surfacing aquatic reptile or mammal. Although filtered through the soothing sound canopy of whistling birds and buzzing insects, the sudden, insulting grunt of a hippopotamus brings a trepidating reminder that this vaguely comical animal takes the lives of more humans than any other beast in Africa.

A malachite kingfisher on an overhanging twig cocks its head in search of small bream in the water below, its iridescent back reflecting the brilliant sky. Spotting a cichlid, the diminutive bird drops like a stone, traps the fish in its long, red bill, and ascends wet-winged back to its perch, fluttering to dry off.

After beating the bill-clenched fish into submission against a branch, the kingfisher swallows it head-first. Satisfied, but still hungry, the bird resumes its vigil.

Screeching with intent, an African fish eagle leaps from high in a leafless leadwood tree and swoops down over the water. The black, white and reddish raptor lowers its landing gear, then spreads its talons and locks onto a floating tigerfish. Struggling to regain altitude with this sudden added load, the eagle climbs slowly back into the sky, settling once again on its lofty perch to feed.

A pair of pygmy geese flush out of the water, their whistling wings setting off concentric rings of ripples. They flap across tall stalks of papyrus on their way to a nesting

Striding across the bone-dry ground at the perimeter of the delta, a chameleon watches for insects—which it snaps up in a blink with a body-long tongue.

cavity in the hollow of a leadwood tree. The female is midway through her 24-day incubation period. On the day after her 10 white eggs hatch, she will lead the youngsters to water. During the two-month period they need to mature, most of the goslings will fall prey to crocodiles, turtles and tigerfish.

Tiptoeing on splayed feet across lily pads, an African jacana bows deftly here and there to snap up insects, its open wings shifting like the balancing pole of a high-wire acrobat. Nestled in the nearby floating vegetation are the bird's four eggs, their scrawled brown coloring their only camouflage.

Ahead of the mokoro, there is the splash of two shy sitatungas—long-legged, supple-hooved antelope well suited to running in the marshes. Their twisted horns held back over their shoulders, they flow like brown rivulets through the green, swampy landscape, then seemingly melt into the reeds.

What appear to be rounded rocks in the distance are actually a scrum of 15 hippopotamuses. As the mokoro approaches, one of the largest of the herd slowly swings open its cavernous maw, showing off teeth like rail spikes that are stained yellow from years of grazing on marsh grasses. Holding this yawn far longer than needed to threaten, the hippopotamus finally slams closed its maw, then grunts an authoritative, disapproving "hoo, hoo, hoo." As it submerges indignantly, the waters rush to fill the vacuum left by its rotund body.

Migrating impalas and zebras mingle in harmony through the grasslands and forests of the delta.

A consorting pair of lions finds camouflage in the tall grasses on one of the delta's many islands.

Though intimidating, the hippopotamuses play a vital role in the natural engineering of the delta. With their considerable bulk and enormous hooves, they dredge open the channels, permitting the waters to pass and facilitating the flow of fish and animal traffic. Nonetheless, the Mbukushu native cautiously maneuvers the mokoro in a wide arc around this herd and continues on along the channel.

By day the Okavango Delta is a parading pageant of life. The participants are grazers, browsers, insect eaters, fishers and pollen gatherers. Nightfall brings a damper, mustier air and signals the arrival of a second cast of players, their distinctive sounds echoing through the black stillness.

With the coming of darkness, the hippopotamuses haul their hulking bodies out of the water and waddle down ancestral trails to familiar inland grazing sites.

A cat-like, rusty-spotted genet furtively climbs a tree to observe a female Pel's fishing owl emerging from her nest. Procuring food for the two downy youngsters she has left, the tawny-colored mother alights on a stump overhanging the shore and searches for movement of a fish, a frog or a rodent below. Unlike many other types of owls, her legs and feet have no feathers, making them ideal for plucking prey from the water. While waiting, the mother emits a deep "hooommhut," a double-hooted cry intended to reassure the two young owlets. But unless she

returns quickly to the nest, she may lose her offspring to the genet closing in on them.

Adding to the music of the Okavangan night are the ringing, throaty calls of painted reed frogs and the incessant percussions of clacking, buzzing and sawing insect choruses. Strutting behind his pride of lionesses on the trail of a Cape buffalo, a male lion roars, then grunts four times.

Not heard in the bawdy blackness is the emperor moth that as a caterpillar ate the leaves of a mopane tree. Nor is the silver-green Moon moth that was weaned from foliage of the marula tree. Both moths flutter silently in the night, testing the air for the pheromones of potential mates.

The blossoms of the female night lily unfold in silent beauty. Overhead squads of Peters' epauletted fruit bats dip quietly to skim a drink on the wing, then head off to seek fig trees and motsaudi berries; they leave colorful droppings as proof of a varied diet.

Rosy-breasted in the sun's light, doves meeting at a water hole seem keener on soaking their feet than quenching their thirst.

Keeping its feet still in the waters, a saddle-billed stork snatches unsuspecting bream.

ABOVE: *A wading jacana steps toe-splayed on lily pads across the waters.* BELOW: *Like bright tree blossoms, carmine bee-eaters perch at a nesting colony.*

Wild and unspoiled, the Okavango Delta is deceptively fragile, threatened by both wildlife and people. Ironically, elephants have become one of the most serious threats to the region's ecosystem. Now numbering some 60,000—more than anywhere else— they are too many for the habitat to support. Not only has the protected local population been increasing naturally, but their ranks have been swollen by migrants from Angola, recently torn by civil war, and from Zambia,

A skulking shadow padding through the twilight shallows, the spotted hyena becomes a marauding scavenger when draped by the velvet cloak of night.

which is still a poaching haven. Every day each elephant consumes about 300 pounds of greenery and drinks roughly 50 gallons of water, a heavy demand that has exacted a severe toll. Some areas of the delta have come to look like a war zone.

There are also the problems associated with Botswana's human population, which stands at 1.4 million and is growing at one of the highest rates in Africa. With 95 percent of the land too dry to support crops, there is continuing pressure to tap the waters of the Okavango Delta. One plan—on hold pending further study—calls for dredging 25 miles of one main channel and increasing the outflow by a projected 50 million cubic meters of water per year. The supply would serve Maun, the closest town, and Orapa, a center of the diamond mining that accounts for 80 percent of the nation's export earnings.

The threat of cattle overrunning the delta is ever-present as well. Considered a measure of wealth by Botswanans, they outnumber humans by a margin of about two to one. Until recently, the delta was for the most part off limits to both cattle and people because of the risk of deadly diseases. Sleeping sickness, carried by the tsetse fly—called "the best game warden in Africa"—and foot-and-mouth disease, carried by the Cape buffalo, together made a formidable barrier. In the 1950s the building of a barricade known as the "Buffalo Fence" was begun along the southwest edge of the delta, chiefly to keep

in disease-carrying Cape buffalo; an indirect, beneficial consequence was to keep out cattle altogether. But the spraying of pesticides has dramatically lessened the danger of disease, prompting the call for allowing cattle to graze within the borders of the delta.

Meanwhile, more and more adventure-seeking travelers—currently about 33,000 annually—are drawn to this Eden of wilderness. Tourism has become the number one

source of jobs for northern residents. Some 50 camps of tents, thatched cottages and houseboats have sprung up. Flying safaris based in Maun hopscotch from camp to camp, while ground tours are conducted in safari vans and huge four-wheel-drive trucks.

Yet compared to many of its neighbors—Kenya, for example, attracts 600,000 tourists a year—Botswana basks in relative seclusion, still not easily reached, far from being tamed.

Elsewhere elephants and other species face extinction, their numbers greatly depleted by unrestrained poaching. However, Botswana can be credited with concerted efforts at wildlife protection and conservation. A growing establishment of environmentalists and a government receptive to safeguarding the nation's unique natural heritage are encouraging signs for the Okavango Delta, the jewel in the crown of wildest Africa.

*M*Y FIRST TRIP TO THIS COASTAL DESERT OF *southwest Africa was in the late 1950s, after an expedition to Etosha National Park about 100 miles to the east across the Kaokoveld. I returned in 1985 and again in 1987. By then, the government of Namibia had established the Skeleton Coast National Park, a strip of protected sands about 300 miles long and 25 miles wide.*

The Skeleton Coast chafes with its scratchy dryness; the taste of grit lingers long on the throat after each parched swallow. The riverbeds are little more than rocky ravines. Occasional springs feed modest pools that sparkle with the blues and greens of dissolved mineral particles.

Nearly all life in the region, from plants to grazing animals, owes its existence to condensation brought by almost-daily banks of fog—the main source of moisture. An early-morning blessing, the fog results from a meeting of warm, moist air with the cold of the northbound Benguela Current offshore; it can drift 60 miles inland.

Yet, I was astounded by the variety of wildlife: gemsbok and springbok, mountain zebra, kudu, ostrich. Most surprising were the black rhinos, giraffes and elephants. On my first trip I saw lions prowl the beaches, preying on seals that they would kill and drag inland. Sadly, they are now gone, victims of hunting outside the protected desert borders by poachers and livestock-defending herdsmen.

Rhinos wandering from the east into what is now the Skeleton Coast faced extinction in the 1970s, poached for their horns which were used as dagger handles and in medicinal potions. But in an experimental conservation program that started in the late 1980s, living rhinos have had their horns sawed off to discourage poachers, and are now under study for how this affects them.

When I came here in the 1950s the western Kaokoveld was home to more than 300 elephants. They would troop

The Skeleton Coast is a 300-mile strip of defiant desert fringing the Atlantic shores of Namibia.

across dunes, some of which were hundreds of feet high, and charge down to the coastal shores to play in the surf. Their ranks have been cut to about 80, most of this loss at the hands of indigenous people in the region. Fortunately, though, their numbers seem to be increasing again.

My last trip here was to help regional officials with a study of elephants. Leading the expedition was an experienced game catcher and former park warden. (Earlier in his career, he had provided the animals and set up the stunts and chase scenes for a classic African movie called HATARI!, which starred John Wayne.) Instead of immobilizing a baby elephant with a tranquilizer in order to tag it, he had a plan that he believed was more humane: Sneak up on a herd and storm into the middle, cull a baby—like a quarter horse cutting a calf—tag it, then get out fast! A film crew was on hand with me to shoot footage of him putting his theory into practice.

A problem with our leader's fast-in, fast-out approach was that some areas in the open plains of the Kaokoveld are strewn with boulders the size of basketballs. Walking there is difficult, much more so overtaking a thundering herd of elephants in a Land Cruiser that is airborne half the time from bouncing. But he was convinced his plan would work.

From their helicopter, our scouts spotted a herd of 40 to 50 elephants, and we set off after them in two Land Cruisers; the one that I was in would do the chasing, the other would do the filming. We quickly discovered that trying to sneak up on a herd of elephants in the desert is next to impossible. They saw us coming, broke and ran. Negotiating the boulders was no challenge for them, but for us meant quite a ride. Our Land Cruiser almost threw out the crew in the back, and would have launched me through the roof of the cab had I not been strapped down securely in my seat.

With some fancy driving, we caught up to the herd—much to my surprise. I had never thought I would find myself lurching 40 miles an hour through a herd of squealing, trumpeting elephants, chewing clouds of dust and dizzied by the roar of engines. The Land Cruiser circled around so close to some bulls that I could almost reach out and touch them.

I happened to look up at one point to see that a female of the herd had turned around and was charging back toward us. As we veered to our right, the elephant veered to its left and nearly collided with us, then sat down on the Land Cruiser, crushing the hood and landing almost in my lap! I was saved by a few precious inches of crumpled metal.

We called off the chase for the day and regrouped the following morning. This time, one of the front wheels fell off the Land Cruiser and we were jolted to an inglorious halt in the middle of the herd. But on our next foray, we succeeded in culling a baby. Some baby it was: a feisty four-year-old, already about four feet tall at the shoulder. Eleven of us had to hold it while it was quickly tagged.

By the time we had finished, we were reconsidering our options. Although the elephants seemed to have fared well, our approach had ended up being rough on man and machine—and nearly ended my career. I could imagine the reaction back home. "Did you hear about poor Fowler? An elephant sat on him. What a way to go!"

—JF

SKELETON COAST

BY BERN KEATING

Perhaps no place on earth is more fearsomely named than southwest Africa's Skeleton Coast, a desolate landscape well-deserving of its intimidating moniker. Few sites in the world loom more hostile to life.

But the Skeleton Coast also thrills with a contrary miracle. Here, every element of geography and climate dictates death, yet life improbably exists—and even flourishes.

Occupying a 300-mile strip of Atlantic shoreline along the west of Namibia, the Skeleton Coast lays stubborn claim to territory from Swakopmund in the south to the Kunene River at the border of Angola in the north. Although its politically sanctioned boundaries enclose an area of about 6,500 square miles—larger than Connecticut and Rhode Island put together—the wasteland sprawls well beyond its furthest designated inland limit of 25 miles. The thirsting, outstretched arm of the Namib, reputedly one of the world's oldest and driest deserts, it receives an average rainfall of barely half an inch annually—perhaps as much as an inch in a generous year. And even this miserly trickle is rationed, arriving in sporadic drizzles, most of which are hardly measurable.

Until recently, the region went by the drably deceptive tag of Kaokoveld Coast. "Skeleton Coast," the story goes, was first coined in 1933 by a journalist as a way to identify the suspected crash site of a missing aircraft. It was an apt description for this sandswept shoreline graveyard, which is littered with the skeletal remains of ships, planes, whales and humans—some of them mysteriously headless. So the name took hold. (The unfortunate pilot, however, like many others who came to the coast before him, was never heard from again.)

Since the earliest days of its exploration, the Skeleton Coast has been a mariner's horror. Vengeful currents savage the shores, disfiguring features until the face of the land is unrecognizable. The protected harbors of one generation are lost to the next. Shoals and sandbars appear and disappear, never recorded on charts. For part of virtually every day, blinding fog makes even sight of the shores impossible. Navigating the treachery is still a formidable challenge with today's sophisticated seafaring technology.

Cast-ashore victims confront an uncharitable land, one that is at best cruelly indifferent to human needs. Nonetheless, the Skeleton Coast's twin, parallel environmental zones—the beach and the interior—teem with surprising vibrancy, their extraordinarily adaptive life forms having learned to outwit conditions that are harsh beyond the extremes of the imagination.

Hot winds whip the sands into sultry dunes, their breathtaking poses insinuating an ethereal eroticism—especially when they are seen from the air. Garnet crystals sit like crowns atop their crests and tumble in fancy arabesques down their sleek slopes. Marked on the map are rivers that empty into the

Stirring sands appear to swallow mountain zebras as they sprint toward rocky hills in the interior.

Two combative seas—one ocean water, one desert sand—butt along the shifting scrimmage of Skeleton Coast's shoreline.

Atlantic Ocean, but here the search for them is in vain. Their waters soak out of sight into the sands long before they reach the sea, escaping to it through channels underground. Above the subterranean streams, green stretches of linear oasis rise stoically along the dry beds, their riverine vegetation the harvest of gazelles, giraffes, or the occasional desert-dwelling elephants and mountain zebras that wander in from the eastern reaches of the interior. The rare water holes are frequented by surviving black rhinoceroses, thick-skinned eluders of the poachers who have threatened their existence.

Lions, also hunted to virtual extinction, no longer venture to the coast to scavenge for dead seals. But springbok and gemsbok still abound, along with kudu—gray-brown, spiral-horned antelopes. Almost everything that moves, even the lowly termite, is prey to the black-backed jackals and brown hyenas that prowl the sands. Ostriches, seemingly oblivious, frolic gaily among the shifting dunes in flocks of as many as 20.

Just offshore rolls the mighty Benguela Current, a frigid deep-sea torrent that originates thousands of miles away in the ice-steeped Antarctic. Coming to grief against the resolute land mass of southwest Africa, the vindictive current boils to the surface, stealing heat from the air along the obstructing shores that divert it north. Warm, moist morning winds from the west, stung by the chilly reception that greets them as they

FAR LEFT: *Young bull seals contest a rocky stretch of beach.*
NEAR LEFT: *Like a confused pack of sightseers far from home, jackass penguins parade the southern shores.*

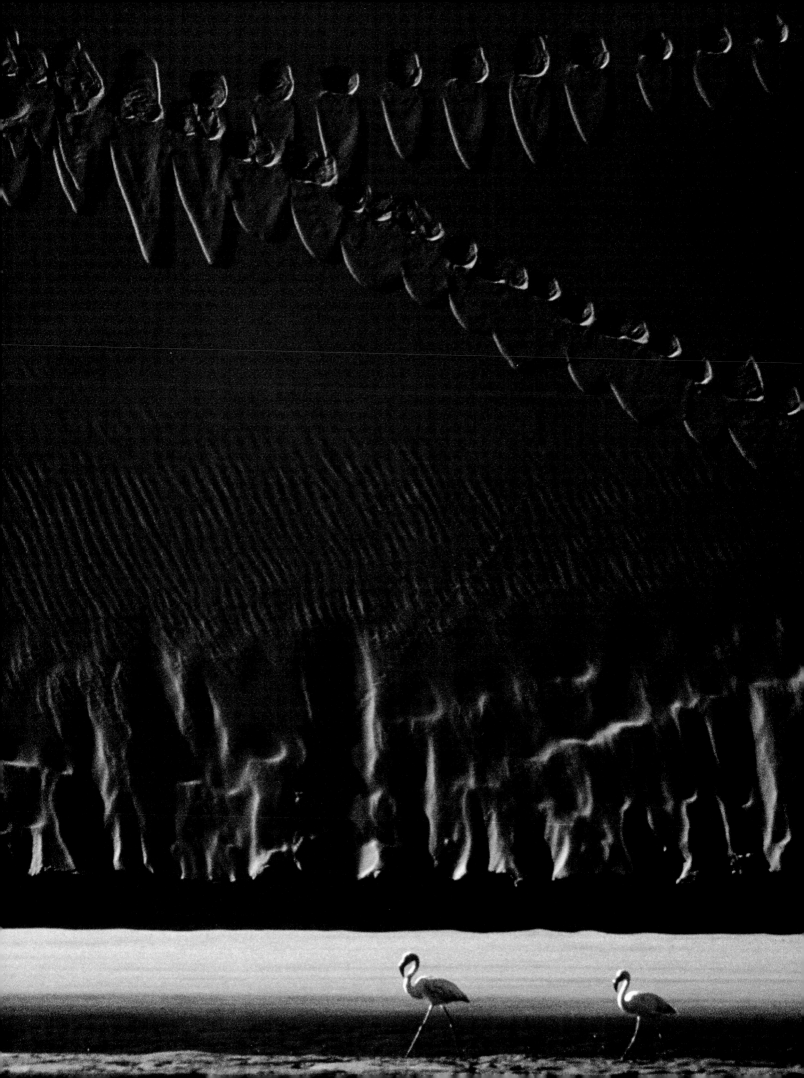

RIGHT: *As part of their
courtship ritual, gannets
strike a sky-pointing display.*

LEFT: *Flamingos stoop before
a desert dune as if taking
bows at a coastal curtain call,
flushed by rippling applause
from the waters.*

approach the coast, dump their rains futile-ly into the sea. Only the dregs drift east to the shores, spilling as a thick, sweaty fog that spreads inland for 30 to 60 miles; by mid-morning, however, the blistering sun will have burned it all away.

For the Skeleton Coast, the climatic out-come is a bewildering paradox of almost constant humidity and virtually no rainfall. Contrary to widespread belief, temperatures along the beaches seldom rise above 90°F. The exception, oddly enough, is in winter, when the hot bergwind blowing from the inland desert in the east overpowers the cool air offshore; then, the sands along the coast can skyrocket by midday to a searing 150°F.

The Benguela Current, which on the one hand deprives the land of much-needed rain, on the other hand supports an immense population in the sea. With each upwelling, it showers the surface waters with a wealth of minerals to nourish vast, hungry mead-ows of plankton. Fat, foamy rolls of plank-ton that are nearly a mile long sweep ashore with the west wind; these yard-thick scuds of green scum plaster the dunes, nursing the tinder-dry roots of vegetation that clings to life in the sands. The rich bounty of the sea also feeds a thriving fish population, which includes cob, galjoen, steenbra and blacktail. Overhead, shrieking marine birds alternate-ly soar and dive, effortlessly plucking their slippery catch from the teeming waters. Terns and cormorants are but two of the more than 200 species that can be found here; as well, there are many polar migrants, along with waders such as plovers, turn-stones, sanderlings and little stints.

The whales that once churned the salty mead are gone, victims of relentless hunting a century ago. Their bleaching bones, half-buried on the beach, rise from the sands like

RIGHT: *Looking like a crash-survivor from another planet, the welwitschia lives for centuries.* RIGHT, BELOW: *A mature milk bush sprouts unusual new growth of bright green.*

The gemsbok endures years of drought on the moisture of eaten foliage.

mournful memorials, interspersed among the rusting plates and rotted ribs of dashed ships and aircraft that mark the fateful passing of misguided mortals. Near Cape Cross in the south, two incongruously out-of-place monuments vie awkwardly for the right to recall Diego Câo, a Portuguese navigator who came ashore here in 1486 on an unsuccessful search for a sea route to India and the Spice Islands.

However, a colony of fur seals nearby and another at Cape Fria in the north show that life goes on. Here the bubbling waters literally burst with their bobbing heads and

hungry barking. Yet, for all their inviting playfulness, they are possibly most memorable for their excruciating halitosis—their breath testimony to the some 35 pounds of fish, octopus, squid and rock lobsters that they can consume each day.

Threatened in the past by hunters seeking their pelts, oil and meat, the seals are once again so numerous that the colony must be culled from time to time. Indeed, the pups are lucky to escape a crushing by the bulls, which are heedless of their 500- to 600-pound bulk. Neglected by their parents, the dead and dying are vulnerable to the

RIGHT: *Driven off by the withering coastal dryness, gemsbok drift to the rocky inland plains in search of short-lived vegetation born of a rare thunderstorm.*

OVERLEAF: *Sand-skirted dunes dance across the desert floor, their swirling pleats crisply sun-dried and wind-pressed.*

jackals and hyenas that often wander unchallenged through the nursery, sometimes having their pick of the unguarded healthy as well. Not surprisingly, survivors assume the perils of the sea on their own while yet very young. Still, no more than 25 percent of the pups reach maturity.

Along the northern stretch of coast, the deep-throated morning fog seems to swallow all sound. The thick air clings as if afraid, not daring to break the silence. Neither the shrill cry of a shore bird nor the stitch of an insect carries far. Distorted by the refracting mist, the shifting dunes look menacing; they become looming hulks of nightmarish scale and proportion. Suddenly, there is the unsettling, building roar of an avalanche as cascading sands ripple slowly down from the peak of a steep slope.

Looking very much at home, however, a rakish ganna shrub sits peacefully rooted on top of a dune—which the plant actually played a role in building. Beginning as a tiny seedling, the ganna used its small, crumbly leaves to catch particles of sand blowing in the wind. By dropping them on its sheltered lee, the plant initiated the forming of the dune. As the sand piled higher in the wind, the plant grew too, slithering out roots just

below the surface of the mound and combing the wind for ever more grains to add to its castle. Another shrub, the naras, erects towering dunes up to 180 feet high in much the same manner; its roots push to depths of 45 feet in search of underground moisture.

Marvels at recycling, these crafty plants also stock a larder on their sheltered, leeward sides. Trapping the decaying crumbs of animals and plants carried by the wind, they gather bits of insect legs and carapaces, with-

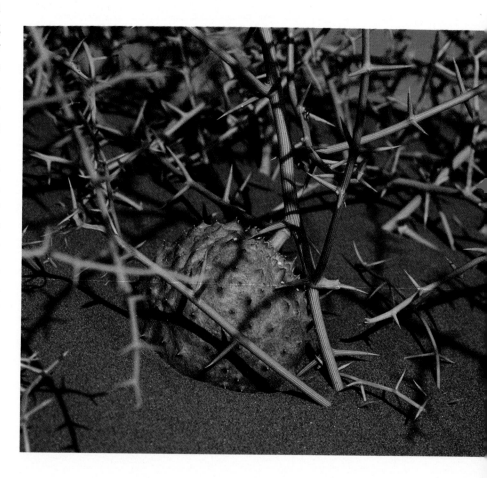

The naras shrub stands on thorny guard as if protecting its gourd from grazing robbers such as the gemsbok.

ABOVE: *A scorpion mother coddles her newborn offspring.* ABOVE, RIGHT: *Dripping with dew, a tenebrionid beetle licks up precious dribbles.*

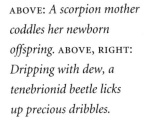

ered leaves, twigs and fungus. Raiding beetles and other insects dig out of the sands to plunder this detritus, only to become food for lizards and snakes. The reptiles, in turn, are the fattened prey of birds and jackals, which deposit manure to nourish the plants.

The almost-daily fog is a blanket of moist mercy over all the gritty dryness. Fleshy, hairy leaves of succulents crib tiny droplets out of the misty air. Some plants stretch the fine threads of their roots outward through the sands to coax in dribbles from the surface. Other plants thrust roots deep into the sands to soak up moisture from damp pockets underground.

Odd and strikingly inventive plants populate this banished colony of garden marginals. The red-flowered *Hoodia macrantha* riffles its purple hairs as if breathing lustily. In the cause of reproduction, the plant emits a stench of rotting meat to entice unsuspecting female insects. They are fooled into thinking that their larvae will feast on carrion and lay their eggs in vain, unwittingly picking up fertile pollen that they then supply to the next stink-alluring plant along their path. Unquestionably one of the most grotesque plants in the world is the bushman's buttocks (*Lithops ruschiorum*), a succulent as pink as the gravel in which it grows and plainly suggestive of its common name. A yellow bud that blooms boldly from an inglorious spot is the ungracious thanks it gives for the doting drizzles of April and May.

A bold survival strategy, different from that adopted by most plants in the region, works extremely well for the welwitschia, a dwarf tree with only two leathery, wind-shredded leaves. While other plants restrict the size of their leaves to minimize the loss of precious moisture through pores, welwitschias sprout large, untidy leaves with millions of pores that suck misty drops out of the morning fog. In addition, their water-divining roots can plumb to a depth of 20 feet. Among the oldest forms of life found anywhere in the world, the welwitschia is indeed successful: In an environment where humans depend on outside support to last more than a few days, it can endure for as long as 2,000 years.

During the rare, brief shower of rain on the dunes, the valleys—called streets—swell in a frenzied explosion of life. Plants that have been dormant for 10 years or more frantically germinate and scatter seeds on the sandy floor. Zebra grasses hastily sprout hairy blades of bright, vibrant green. Giddy shaving-brush grasses stand empty-headed, their glossy seeds strewn in the air and blowing into clusters of fluffy, silver balls. Eight-day grasses germinate and flower at the speed for which they are named, racing to spill the seeds of another generation. The wait for the next rain to launch this celebratory cycle may last for 15 years.

Eighty percent of the grasses are quickly consumed by greedy termites, themselves a

dietary staple to birds, lizards, scorpions, jackals, hyenas and meerkats. Moisture-crazed insects and reptiles reproduce feverishly, gerbils at a dizzying rate that only they can sustain. Bustards the size of turkeys fly from the interior to feast on prey that has grown careless, having lived so long in the predator-free dryness.

Hungry gemsbok are among the beasts that come to sample the revived vegetation. A lion or two may wander from far in the eastern interior to stalk them, but their yard-long rapier-like horns make them formidable prey. Stoically withstanding even the hottest of days, the gemsbok are blessed with networks of capillaries in their noses that cool their blood before it reaches their brains. Like the occasional giraffes that can be spotted at a riverine oasis, they absorb most of their moisture by eating fog-soaked leaves and seldom need to drink.

Some predators of the Skeleton Coast rely almost exclusively on the body juices of their prey for life-giving moisture. One of them is the Namib wasp, which stings and paralyzes an unsuspecting spider, then lays a single egg on the subdued captive and buries it alive for the larva to feed on.

When fog descends on the dunes, entire communities of ants appear from their shelters in the sands. As drops of moisture condense on their bodies, they lick their fill off each other's backs. Some types of tenebrionid beetles emerge to dig trenches across the path of the mist-laden winds. Taking their places along the leeward lips of the trenches, they suck up drips that condense and dribble down the walls. Other beetles that are known as headstanders climb a crest of sand, then turn their backs to the wind and deftly stand on their heads—a feat that allows drops to condense on their shiny carapaces and run down into their awaiting, open mouths.

Too soon, the morning's veil of fog lifts in submission to the spoiling sun, leaving the sands to the torturing, hot-fisted blows of drying winds. Then, life itself appears to forsake the Skeleton Coast. Within hours, even the tracks of the retreating are wiped from the desert floor; all that remain are the chalky imprints left by the heavy-footed on the gravel flats between dunes.

The world's oldest and deepest lake and largest body of fresh water, Lake Baikal fills a 395-mile-long rift-formed basin in Siberia.

*I*N THE SPRING OF 1987 I SPENT two weeks with an American-Soviet crew in this region of central Siberia. We were filming a rafting expedition through the rugged Altay Mountains on the Katun, a river that flows into the mighty Ob.

Our hosts were well organized and attentive, focusing strictly on the duties at hand during our busy days negotiating the river. But as we gathered around the campfire in the evenings, they would engage us in spirited discussions on a wide range of subjects.

One topic they brought up time after time was Lake Baikal. Cradled by forested mountains in the interior, this great body of fresh water is a revered treasure. They referred to it as "the Sacred Sea," "the Pearl of Siberia" and the last, most magnificent "jewel of wilderness." I heard it likened to the Grand Canyon, and in some ways I must agree with the comparison: Both are natural wonders nearly too vast to comprehend and each one possesses a subtle beauty that defies easy description.

Lake Baikal is indeed a marvel. Not only is it the world's oldest and largest lake, it is also the deepest, dropping more than a mile from its surface to its bed. I have read that the total outflow of all the rivers in the world would take about a year to fill the lake's rift-formed basin. Scientists recently discovered thermal vents on the lake bed—a sign of powerful tectonic forces at work—and have learned that the warm currents from these vents nurture sponges and other exotic freshwater life forms. Half of the many hundreds of species of plants and animals living in the lake's waters are found nowhere else in the world. The nerpas, for example, are the only freshwater seals. The golomyanka, an oily fish that is almost transparent, bears live young.

Our fellow rafters, however, preferred to talk about Bigfoot. Believing that a Siberian version of this hairy man-ape roams the mountains west of Lake Baikal, they badgered us with questions about the Bigfoot that reputedly dwells in the western mountains of North America. Did we think one exists? Had we ever seen one?

They also told us of a legendary monster, like the fabled creature of Loch Ness, that prowls the depths of Lake Baikal. Who knows? It is a strange place where seals wind up 2,000 miles from the nearest salt water.

As well, we heard tales about the miracle health properties of Lake Baikal. According to one story, someone who puts a hand in the water will live an extra five years. Putting a leg in adds a further decade. And a person brave enough to swim the frigid waters can count on another 25 years—if, that is, he survives the probable heart attack!

Sad to say, however, veneration of the lake did not stop the building of a massive pulp plant on its shores in the 1960s. (A 1987 government promise that the plant would be retooled and put to non-polluting use seems unlikely to be kept in the foreseeable future.) And in the last 30 years there has been other development: coal-fired power plants, factories and so on. A cellulose plant was what our companions—and apparently most people of the region—held in highest contempt, condemned as a disgusting monstrosity that is fouling their "Sacred Sea." Since the waters of Lake Baikal are still pure enough to drink in all but a few locations, some might consider such vehemence an overreaction. However, the passion of the local people should serve as a reminder that wilderness cannot ever be taken for granted, that everyone shares responsibility for it.

—JF

LAKE BAIKAL

BY BOYD NORTON

From the window of a spacecraft, Lake Baikal appears as an unblinking eye peering out of the mountain-rimmed fastness of south central Siberia. A curved crescent of blue, it has greater volume than any other lake, holding 20 percent of the earth's liquid fresh water. For more than 25 million years—this is also the oldest lake—it has been staring back at the cosmos as if witness to the very soul of the planet. Plunging to depths of more than 5,700 feet, Lake Baikal stakes its claim as the deepest lake as well, and a four-mile layer of sediment that pads its bottom means that the total drop to the underlying bedrock is more than five miles.

Most lakes are transitory things on the endlessly patient time scale of geology. In the northern hemisphere many are the products of continental glaciation, leftovers from the last Ice Age that will eventually silt up and evaporate as their waters become shallower. Even the Great Lakes of North America are expected to vanish in a million years or so.

But Lake Baikal is different. Geological forces guarantee its existence well beyond its present age, for it is situated in the heart of a rift zone, one not unlike Africa's Great Rift. Tectonic plates pulling apart at the rate of almost an inch a year assure that the Baikal rift will grow wider and deeper. The region is one the world's most seismically active, with earthquakes occurring every few hours of the day. Fortunately, most of the tremors are so small that they pass virtually unnoticed.

Only the deepest of secrets can hide in the clear waters off Marble Beach.

Thanks to Lake Baikal's longevity, some of its life forms have evolved into species found nowhere else in the world. In this immense and rich biological broth, more than 1,200 unique types of plants and animals make their home. Among them are such oddities as fish-eating flatworms over a foot long, bright green sponges that would seem more at home in the Caribbean or Red Sea, and scaleless, nearly transparent fish called golomyanka that bear their young live rather than laying eggs. The golomyanka reach lengths of about eight inches and derive their remarkable translucency from the body oil that comprises more than a third of their weight. Well-adapted to the chilly depths of the lake, they rise up to the surface at night to feed on amphipods and other zooplankton. With the warming rays of sunlight at dawn, they descend once again, for they cannot survive long at temperatures higher than 45°F.

Biologists attribute the superb natural quality of Lake Baikal's water to a tiny crustacean called *Epischura baicalensis*. Beneath a single square yard of the lake's surface there are likely to be as many as three million of these creatures. Miniature shrimp, they feed on plankton, algae and bacteria, purging the waters of potential turbidity and producing a clarity for which the lake has become legendary. A shiny kopek that is tossed over the side of a boat remains visible for as much as a hundred feet as it drops into the abyss.

Nerpas, the world's only freshwater seals, loll in the sun at Tonkii Island.

Surprisingly, life exists all the way down to the very bottom of Lake Baikal. For aquatic animals to survive, there must be an adequate supply of oxygen dissolved in the waters. In Africa's Lake Tanganyika, second deepest in the world at 4,708 feet, life disappears below 600 feet. Because of the tropical climate, waters warmed by the sun stay close to the surface; with little mixing, the deeper waters are stagnant and devoid of life. But by virtue of its chilly Siberian locale, the waters of Lake Baikal mix thoroughly, carrying dissolved oxygen even to the greatest depths. The cooled, life-giving surface waters sink, creating convections and promoting circulation—a process that is aided by thermal vents on the lake bottom. Further contributing to the mixing cycle are 336 cold, clear rivers and streams that flow into the lake, most of them fed by melting snows in the surrounding mountains.

Possibly the most enigmatic of Lake Baikal's endemic species is the nerpa, the world's only freshwater seal. A relative of the Arctic ringed seal, the nerpa has been isolated from the nearest ocean for thousands of years. Scientists believe that sometime during the last Ice Age—about 12,000 years ago— the Arctic Ocean reached much farther south than it does today. The seals may have been pushed southward by advancing glaciers, then migrated, first up the Yenesei River and later along the Angara River, which is Lake Baikal's only outlet. Eventually, they wound

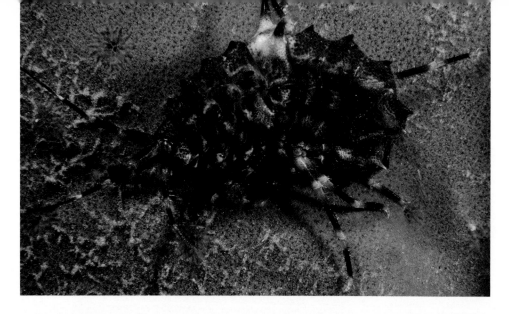

Straying off algae-covered rocks to graze on sponges, an amphipod loses its camouflage.

Morning's light parts a curtain of clouds over the Bay of Ayaya.

Unlikely inhabitants of fresh water, branching sponges rise from beds as much as 60 feet deep.

OVERLEAF: *Heavy storm clouds hover over the bay of Maloye Morye—which in English means "Little Sea."*

The translucent golomyanka feeds by night on zooplankton near the lake surface.

up in this other "ocean," albeit one that is a sea of fresh water.

The nerpas were not the only migrants forced to relocate by the glaciers. Another of the species unique to Lake Baikal is a tasty fish called omul, a member of the salmonid family. The forerunners of the omul are believed to have followed the same river route to Lake Baikal as did the incipient stock of nerpas. Today, the omul is a supplement to the golomyanka in the basic diet of the lake seals.

As creatures of the salty sea, the seals had to contend with killer whales, for whom they were a favored dietary staple. In Lake Baikal, however, they have no marine predators. Here, danger takes the form of wolves and brown bears that roam the shorelines to prey on sunning nerpas. In order to survive the hot days of summer, the seals have learned to congregate on the Ushkanyi Islands off the lake's northeast shore, land that is now a part of Zabaikalsky National Park. Isolated here from the mainland predators, they can bask in relative safety.

As another concession to the threat of terrestrial predators, the nerpas give birth to their young in the bitterly cold months of

February and March, a time when the brown bears are hibernating. Waters beneath the ice hold at a nearly constant 38°F. throughout the winter. Air temperatures, however, are known to plunge below -40°F. Thanks to their oil-heavy diet of golomyanka, the nerpas store an insulating layer of fat to guard against this imperiling deep freeze. The pregnant female digs a cave in a snowdrift on the frozen lake. Nearby, the male keeps open a hole in the three-foot-thick ice to allow passage for feeding. Nursed on fat-enriched milk, the pups acclimatize quickly to the extreme temperatures.

Spring blankets the Baikal basin with warmth, thawing and fracturing the thick winter skin of snow and ice. The winds of mid-May cast the remains of the ice floe in blue heaps along the 1,200 miles of shoreline. And, once again, Lake Baikal becomes a vast expanse of open water. Although the moun-

tains that nearly encircle the lake are still washed in winter whites, the forests that outline the shores take on the cheerful glow of the rhododendron blooms that illuminate the green-darkened conifers.

At Peschanaya Bay on the western shore, in the heart of Pribaikalsky National Park, spring flares like a wildfire. Bursting into flame on the sandy beach, blazing blossoms of red and purple sear into the forests. To the north, at Babushka Bay, the curving beach is swept up in crimson. Midway through the month of June the flowers wither, and calm greens reclaim the forests.

Lake Baikal's wooded perimeter is part of the Siberian taiga, the world's largest contiguous forest. Stretching more than 3,000 miles, from the Ural Mountains in the west to the Seas of Japan and Okhotsk in the east, the taiga is made up of both deciduous and non-deciduous trees to suit the wide variety

Ground cover chokes the eastern shores along Chivyrkuisky Bay.

Cruising the sky at altitudes of up to 200 feet, an osprey searches for fish in the waters below.

The energy-conscious lynx weighs the likely gain from capturing prey against the effort lost in giving chase.

of microclimates that are taken up within its enormous expanse.

Along Lake Baikal's western shores, pine, larch and birch stand in roughly equal proportions. Birch predominate in wet areas, alongside streams and ponds, while pine and larch are more numerous at higher elevations and along rocky cliffs.

However, the mountains tower so high above the lake's surface—in places rising several thousand feet—that they exert a weather influence of their own. At Olkhon Island, the largest isle in Lake Baikal (and reputed to be the burial ground of Mongol conqueror Genghis Khan), a dry microclimate is imposed by the shielding effect of the Primorsky Range. As a result, Olkhon Island is semiarid and bristling with grasslands not unlike those in the steppes of Mongolia, 250 miles to the south. At the northwest corner of the island, sand dunes encroach on the only stands of trees.

By contrast, the region's eastern taiga through Zabaikalsky National Park and along the shores of Chivyrkuisky Bay resembles a rain forest. Dense and lush, the trees are draped with lichens and mosses. The spongy ground cover remains so moist that it makes an ideal breeding ground for world-class mosquitoes that dwarf even those found in Alaska.

The terrestrial plants and animals of the region around Lake Baikal are more or less typical of taiga wildlife elsewhere, many of them related to woodland species of North America and northern Europe. A common forest dweller is the elk—actually the species *Alces alces*, known as the moose in North America. This ungainly-looking member of the deer family is remarkably well-adapted to life in the taiga: On legs seemingly too long for its body, it steps easily through the deep snows of winter and wades far into the feeding waters of summer.

Wolves, wolverines, lynxes, martens, and red foxes also share a common heritage with their counterparts in Alaska, Canada and Scandinavia. But the species for which Lake Baikal is perhaps most renowned is the sable, a member of the weasel family. Prized for its luxuriant fur, the Barguzin sable—named for the spectacular mountain range and river valley east of the lake—was nearly hunted to extinction at the end of the last century. Fearing the demise of a lucrative export, the

ABOVE: *Cracks in the ice that can stretch for a mile or more warn of spring's approach.*

LEFT: *Drifting snows skate across a winter armor of ice three feet thick.*

Russian government created the Barguzinski Zapovednik (Barguzin Nature Reserve) in 1916. It was one of the country's first wildlife refuges. Today, the reserve encompasses a vast region off the northeast shore of Lake Baikal and offers protection to many species of animals as well as plants. With the thought of preserving the splendor of the Barguzin wilds, there is currently talk of extending the reserve to the north or of creating yet another national park.

In the past, remoteness buffered Lake Baikal from the demands of civilization. But with the completion of the Trans-Siberian Railroad in 1904, the lake became vulnerable to development and exploitation. Two quiet Cossack outposts dating back to the 17th century have now become the bustling cities of Irkutsk and Ulan Ude. Together they are home to 900,000 people.

Although the lands surrounding Lake Baikal have remained relatively unspoiled, in the 1960s two pulp plants were put into operation: one at the southern tip of the lake; another along the Selenga River, the lake's largest tributary stream. As a result, there has been pollution of the waters. Fighting against decades of complacency toward the environmental effects on the lake, biologists fear an unraveling of the habitat's intricate web of life. Although different Russian governments have promised to close the plants or convert them to more benign uses, decisive action has been slow to materialize.

With the exception being the careless steps made toward industrialization, Lake Baikal has always been held in highest reverence by the people of the region. To many of the area's early inhabitants, this was the "Sacred Sea," a place imbued with special

A curl of shoreline juts behind Shaman Rock, a craggy outcrop off Olkhon Island.

qualities and powers. In keeping with this tradition of esteem, the lake has become a rallying point for Russia's burgeoning environmental movement. Two national parks were created in 1986 to preserve wilderness shorelines and adjacent lands. Pribaikalsky National Park spans more than half of the western shore, including forested slopes of the Primorsky Range and most of Olkhon Island. On the eastern shore, Zabaikalsky National Park reaches north from the mouth of the Barguzin River to meet the Barguzin Nature Reserve. The boundaries of the park enclose the Holy Nose Peninsula and the Ushkanyi Islands, where the nerpas find sanctuary. Brown bears roam the lonely pebble beaches on the northwest shore, which is the site of the Baikal-Lena Zapovednik, a reserve of rugged peaks that give birth to the Lena River. On the southeast shore, Baikalsky Zapovednik embraces the craggy mountains known as Khamar Daban ("the bear's spine" in native Buryat), which are among the last of the summits in the region to shed the winter's snows.

Although winter is by far the most dramatic of the seasons at Lake Baikal, summer ushers in a surprising warmth and color to the realm. Clear skies and hot sun are the norm for July, with daytime temperatures often jumping to 85°F. or higher. Except in the shallow bays, however, the waters rarely rise above 48°F. By August the broad grassy swales of the Holy Nose Peninsula are alive

Sand dunes encroach on the dwindling woodlands of Olkhon Island.

with the color of wildflowers: purple delphinium and bright crimson *tisachelistnik*, which translates into "plant of one thousand leaves." Elsewhere, the lapping of the waters on the shores seems choreographed by tall, waving blossoms of pink *ivan chai* ("Ivan's tea"), a species related to fireweed, and lavender *podshnezhnik* ("from under the snow").

The brown bears shun the summer heat of the beaches, retreating to the coolness of the taiga and the mountain slopes. There, they feed on ripening berries and, occasionally, on the meat of young or infirm elk that they take down. As summer progresses, the omul and other fish migrate up tributary streams to spawn, and they too become another source of food for the bears. The great bears are laying on body fat for the coming hibernation.

Brisk winds of mid-September portend the return of winter. The birch, aspen and larch glare yellow among the green pines. Within weeks, they are stripped of their leaves, the bare branches rattling in the constricting grip of the cold. Early November sees the first skim of ice forming on the lake—thin, pliable, incredibly transparent. But soon the ice is heavy once again as dense, frigid air settles down heavily on the lake basin. The temperature plunges to -35°F. and may stay there for weeks on end.

Life at Lake Baikal slows to a crawl, but even in the coldest of winters, it never comes to a full stop.

A sad-eyed giant panda bites into crisp stalks of bamboo.

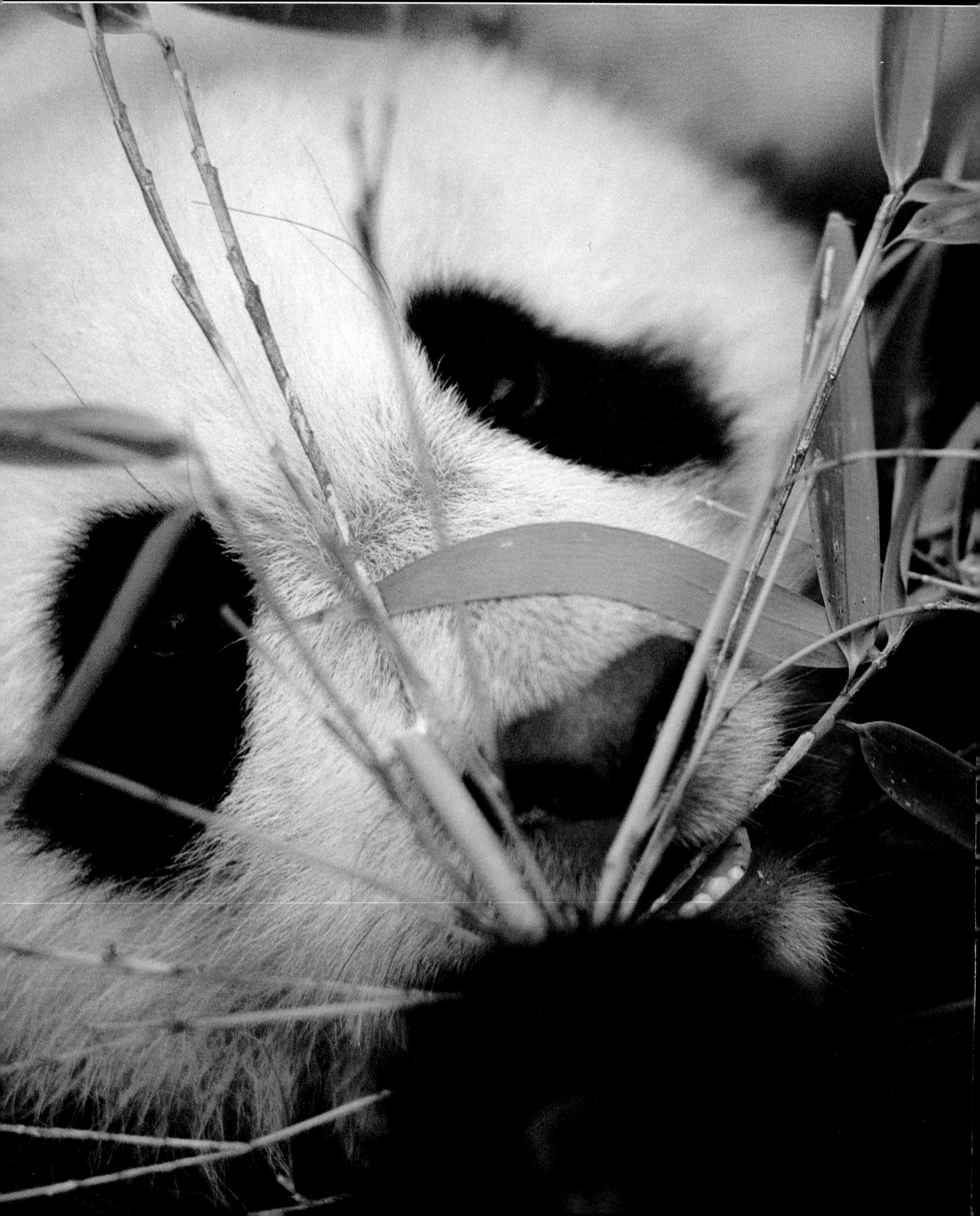

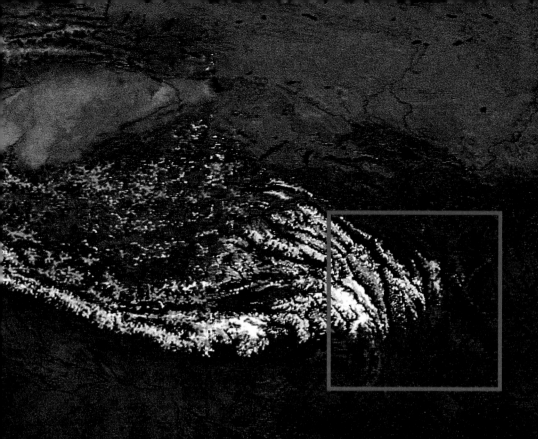

*I*N THE
autumn of
1986 I went to China's Sichuan
Province to see the giant pandas of
the Wolong Natural Reserve. The eastern half of
Sichuan is a flat, agricultural basin. The western
half, by contrast, is a wild and rugged region; situated at the eastern edge of the Tibetan highlands,
its mountains rise abruptly out of the basin.

    During the seven-hour drive west from the city
of Chengdu, I began to get a feeling of déjà vu.
Finally, I realized why: The forested alpine landscape looks very much like parts of the
Rocky Mountains. There are spruces, firs,
hemlocks, birches, maples and other hardwoods, and beneath them rhododendron,
viburnum and laurel. The bamboo was the
obvious difference. Whole slopes were covered
with dense thickets of this woody grass—all the way
up to about 10,500 feet.

    The Wolong forest shelters other creatures in addition
to pandas. The richly varied wildlife includes golden
monkeys, takin, which are cousins to the musk-ox, tufted

A remote region of grassland and dense forest that flanks Daxue Shan, "the Great Snow Mountains," western Sichuan rises from the eastern periphery of a fertile basin of terraced farms that is one of the most heavily populated areas in the world.

deer, golden pheasants, blood pheasants, Darjeeling woodpeckers and some 230 other kinds of birds.

When I reached the reserve, I learned that road crews had been working for six months in preparation for a visit by Prince Philip, head of the World Wildlife Fund. Worried about the decline of the pandas, the Chinese had invited the organization to join in a research and conservation program on the animal that they consider to be a living national treasure.

For a week I bunked in a dormitory near the research center, a collection of low concrete buildings on the western edge of the reserve. The center was built in 1984; it includes a veterinary hospital and a panda nursery. During my stay, I slept on a straw mat in a sleeping bag fashioned from a rough blanket. I wondered if Prince Philip was prepared for the accommodations.

Visibility in bamboo thickets is limited and pandas are skillful at maintaining their privacy. Not surprisingly, the closest I came to any of the creatures in the wild was in hearing their medley of sounds—remarkable assortments of barks, squeals, yips and chirps. But there were a number of the animals that could be observed at the research center, including a mother with a cub the size of a housecat. I noticed how tactile the mother was with her paws, which looked to be as sensitive as hands. She would delicately pick up her cub and hold it against her breast to nurse.

An outdoor compound held a big male panda that was about the

size of a black bear. For special treats, the keeper would give the creature "pig bones," which looked to me like spareribs. I had thought that pandas ate only bamboo, but found out they were originally carnivores and had evolved over time into being principally vegetarians. They developed flat molars for crushing bamboo, and a sixth digit—or false thumb—for grasping the stalks.

The panda in the compound had developed a special bond with his keeper and would follow him around like a dog. Occasionally, however, the animal attacked. The week before my visit the panda had wanted some more meat; when he did not get it, he tore off the keeper's pants.

To get some close-up footage of the panda, the photographer who was with me got down on all fours and crawled to within eight feet of the animal. The panda was sitting back on its haunches, munching bamboo, when all of a sudden he erupted into a rage. I was impressed by how quickly the creature could move. So was the photographer: He dropped his camera and did three backward somersaults! Satisfied that the bluff was successful, the panda went back to eating. I was interested to see that the animal is not the docile plaything that most people imagine them to be.

The panda has become a worldwide symbol of conservation. Saving the shy, elusive creature would mean that other species living in the same forests were also protected. And reaching this goal would heighten world awareness of the need for preserving habitat and species diversity.

—JF

WESTERN SICHUAN

BY GREG STOTT

The word Sichuan usually conjures memories not of a place but of hot, spicy Chinese food. Behind the well-loved cuisine, however, is a land every bit as distinctive as the cooking it sent abroad. The region of Sichuan is China's largest province. It contains some of the most densely populated and intensively cultivated territories on earth—also some of the wildest.

Situated in the southwestern part of the country, the province comprises 219,000 square miles, an area slightly larger than that of France. If Sichuan were an independent country, its 110 million people would make it the world's eighth most populous nation.

Most of the people work the fertile land of the Sichuan Basin, also called the Red Basin because of the terra-cotta hue of the soil. The fields of this ancient growing region have been terraced and irrigated for millennia. Today, there are few agricultural centers that can match Sichuan's output of crops such as rice, wheat, corn and sweet potatoes.

Far from the teeming basin with its hazy, subtropical clime, there is another Sichuan—one that is utterly different. The western reaches of the province climb from the manicured terraces of the farm belt to Daxue Shan, "the Great Snow Mountains," and some of the loftiest, most rugged scenery on earth. Between the two extremes are rain forests and temperate highlands.

The highest pinnacle in Daxue Shan is the 24,784-foot-tall Gongga Shan—Minya

Konka to the Tibetans. According to an inscription found in a mountain monastery, simply gazing at this magnificent summit has the same effect as ten days of meditation. Indeed, the view impressed Joseph Rock, an American who entertained readers of the 1920s and 1930s with accounts of his travels to remote locations. "And then suddenly, like a white promontory of clouds, we beheld the long-hidden Minya Konka," he wrote. "I marveled at the scenery which I, the first white man ever to stand here, was privileged to see. An immense snowy range extended from north to south, and peerless Minya Konka rose high above its sister peaks into a turquoise-blue sky."

In fact, Rock was probably wrong in declaring himself the first westerner ever to set eyes on Gongga Shan (just as he was positively incorrect in calling the mountain the tallest in the world). Rock was justified, however, in his awe of Gongga Shan—an extraordinary sight, even in a land dominated by breathtaking, snow-capped peaks.

In this massive, craggy adjunct to the Himalayas, nature's most prominent works include age-old glaciers, bubbly hot springs, windswept valleys and chiseled canyons alive with the roar of streams. Some of the unruly waters feed the Yangzi, the world's fourth longest river and China's great thoroughfare.

At 10,000 feet and higher, weather-worn Tibetans and their neighboring tribes endure a teeter-totter existence that includes up to

The Pitiao River rushes through a lush, fog-enveloped gorge in the untamed Qionglai Shan.

Ruffles of fungi dress the trunk of a tree in the Sichuan forest.

Today, the sparsely populated region is semi-autonomous, but under Chinese jurisdiction. In the early 1950s, China's governors constructed a road that links the Tibetan capital of Lhasa with Chengdu, the capital of Sichuan. The bone-jarring bus trip between the two cities takes fully two weeks. But along the way there is some of the world's most spectacular scenery. A landmark is the village of Litang, one of the highest settlements in the world. Otherwise, the land seems for the most part untouched by civilization, marked only by packs of domesticated yaks and an occasional Buddhist shrine with prayer flags that ripple in the breeze.

In the Hailuo Valley on the east slope of Gongga Shan, the flora of the Himalayas, China and Japan meet in the forests at the edge of a low-slung glacier that extends four miles down the mountain. There, hot spring waters cascade down the hills among trees that are ten arm's lengths in circumference.

In this Eden, where temperate and subtropical weather patterns mingle in a sort of climatic alchemy, Chinese botanists have counted 5,000 varieties of plants. Perhaps no example better illustrates the astonishing wealth of vegetation than Sichuan's unusually broad sampling of rhododendron. Of the 68 varieties that have been catalogued worldwide, 60 are found only in China; 24 are unique to the region around Gongga Shan.

Western Sichuan is also well endowed in animal species, particularly primates. As is

200 frost days a year and high-altitude sunlight that will blister the skin after a few hours of exposure. In the grasslands of the 15,000-foot-high Kangba Plateau in the far northwest, no sooner do the winter blizzards disappear than the area is wracked by violent lightning storms.

For centuries, this indomitable landscape held the human world at bay. The isolation was reinforced by the influence of feudal warlords and by ongoing conflicts between China and Tibet, which were forever in dispute over the land.

Clinging to the face of a rock, a frog deposits eggs in a sheltered crevice.

the case in many other wilderness strong-holds, however, the future of many of the creatures is anything but certain.

The snow leopard holds court in the upper reaches of the mountains, but not with any real impunity. This exquisite, dense-ly furred feline is still hunted for its pelt or slaughtered for the imagined medicinal ben-efits to be found in its ground-up bones. There have also been attempts to eradicate the cat as a threat to livestock. One estimate puts the number of surviving snow leopards in all of China at no more than 2,000.

Another severely endangered creature is the handsome-coated golden monkey, which thrives among the lichen deposits of the high forests. In staking its survival on life at such extreme elevation, this shy primate has had

ABOVE: *Tree limbs draped with Spanish moss lend a gauzy touch of softness to the Zhon Pin Valley.*

As if to semaphore woodland secrets, an Arisaema *extends hooded, flower-like spathes.*

White, bell-shaped blossoms of rhododendron brighten the spring forest.

to adapt to unusually harsh climatic conditions. At one time, the creature occupied much of eastern China, but its habitat has been dramatically reduced by the demands of agriculture and logging. Today, the golden monkey survives only in wildlife preserves, where it is protected from hunters who kill it for the lush, golden cape that adorns its back and shoulders.

Notwithstanding these extraordinary animals, the rarest and most famous treasure in western Sichuan is the giant panda. This well-loved creature is found—though rarely sighted—in the humid bamboo forests of the central and lower highlands in the region. Like the golden monkey, the panda lives nowhere else, save for a handful of zoos and breeding stations. To the people of many

nations around the world, the animal is familiar as the emblem of the World Wildlife Fund, an organization that has spearheaded efforts to ensure its survival.

With the number of remaining giant pandas hovering around 1,200, the fate of the species teeters on a precipice. This is a starkly discouraging state of affairs, since pandas once wandered a broad swath of eastern China by the tens of thousands. Pandas, in fact, were well known to the Chinese long before the people had refined their skills of agriculture. Fossil records date the animal back as far as three million years, and a 3,000-year-old Chinese text makes mention of the "pi," an early name for the panda.

Giant pandas became known to the outside world far more recently—about the same time that Joseph Rock was first setting eyes on mighty Gongga Shan. Only in the 1930s did rumors of a large bear-like creature of unusual coloring reach Europe and North America. No one at the time, however, had any actual evidence that such an animal indeed existed.

On a rare excursion below the mountain snow line, a summer-coated snow leopard stalks the highland grasses.

Ruth Harkness, a New York socialite, was among those who were deeply smitten with the notion of the creature. She teamed up with a Chinese-American big game hunter, Quentin Young, and in 1936 they trekked through western China in search of the giant panda. By a stroke of good fortune, the team came upon a cub clinging to a tree, hiding from the poachers who had killed its mother. They named the little panda Su-Lin and transported it back to the United States.

Su-Lin stayed at the Harkness apartment before being moved to a Chicago zoo. Sadly, the panda survived for less than a year, succumbing to pneumonia. Prior to the animal's death, public curiosity was fanned incessantly by a media that could never seem to have enough photographs of the engaging creature. Some people even learned from the news accounts that the panda was not, in fact, a bear at all, but a distinct species called *Ailuropoda melanoleuca*.

At the time of Su-Lin's very public death, the human population of Sichuan was close

Extravagantly furred if spiteful in appearance, a golden snub-nosed monkey emerges momentarily from the gloom of the forest.

to 50 million, less than half its current level. The remarkable two-fold increase that has occurred since then is more than just a dramatic statistic: For conservationists, the growth is a warning flare and grim reminder of the enormous pressures that an expanding population exerts on wildlife and natural areas. Even places as remote as western Sichuan cannot be considered immune.

Most of China's population explosion came about during the 1950s and 1960s, when the nation's ideological zeal for growth encouraged logging and the clearing of land for agriculture. The forests of Sichuan, the second largest timber tract in China, were continuously under assault. By the 1980s, the wooded areas had been reduced by more than a third. On the slopes of some mountainous regions of Sichuan, the loss exceeded 60 percent.

As was inevitable, the people of the area have paid a price. Indiscriminate logging severely diminished the water-storage capacities of the forests. In effect, a large portion

LEFT: *Its furry bottom cushioned against the cold, a giant panda rests in the snow as it digs for bamboo.*

of the great natural blotter was destroyed, and massive soil erosion has been the result. Several times, this erosion has contributed to serious flooding of the Yangzi River. In one instance, hundreds of people were killed and more than a million homes were swept away.

Today, the government of China seems to recognize many of the errors made in the past. Some abuses continue—there are still instances of illegal logging, and poaching remains a problem for pandas, snow leopards and golden monkeys. But there appears to have been a profound shift in attitude, at least in official circles, and a great many conservation measures have been enacted. The number of nature reserves in China has risen sharply from 104 in 1981 to more than 700 at

present. Thirteen of these are giant panda reserves in western and northern Sichuan. The same nature parks serve as sanctuaries for other threatened creatures, such as the smaller red panda and the golden monkey.

Wolong, or "Resting Dragon," is the largest of the giant panda reserves, also one of the oldest. Established in the late 1970s and designated as an international biosphere preserve by the United Nations, the 770-square-mile park begins in the foothills just 25 miles northwest of Chengdu.

The 25 miles might as well be several hundred miles, however, for Wolong can only be reached by a long, rather tortuous bus ride. Within the reserve, the pandas live a well-concealed existence, hidden away in

RIGHT: *Well-provisioned on its home turf in the Wolong Natural Reserve, a reed-chewing giant panda dines contentedly.*

ABOVE: *Snow-dusted peaks of the Gankarling Range appear to be coated in flour.*

LEFT: *A distant herd of grass lovers works the gentle flatland along the Yulongshi River.*

thick forests of bamboo. The summer range of pandas extends between elevations of 7,600 and 10,500 feet. Quite at home in the thickets, the pandas spend up to 75 percent of their day consuming enormous quantities of bamboo—typically as much as 30 to 40 pounds each every day. The animals are carnivores as well as herbivores, and they will take meat when they have the opportunity. Such occasions are rare, however, because the pandas are awkward on their feet and ill-suited for the chase.

The fate of these creatures, therefore, depends heavily on their access to bamboo. In a single year, one animal may require as much as five and a half tons of the food—a

fact that renders the protection of surviving forests terribly important. This urgency is heightened by a quirk of nature, which sees large groves of bamboo in western Sichuan blossom and die intermittently. (The intervals usually range from 40 to 120 years.) New growths of bamboo begin when the old ones perish, but scientists worry that an untimely crash in the food supply over a large area might leave many pandas to starve. In the mid-1970s, when a sizable tract of bamboo flowered and withered, 138 pandas died. In 1983, another 100 pandas lost their lives because of a similar occurrence.

In the past decade, the government of China has spent millions of dollars dismantling timber operations near the panda habitats; some farmers have also been required to relocate away from the animal reserves. Moreover, Chinese newspapers report that some 200 people have been arrested for hunting giant pandas, and at least some number of these poachers have been confined to jail. In 1990 two men who were found to be in possession of four panda skins were publicly executed.

Among the nation's 2,094 different types of birds, mammals, reptiles and amphibians, the China Wildlife Protection Association recognizes 98 species as being particularly endangered. For some of this wildlife, nature reserves like Wolong offer at least a hope.

Less than a century ago, western Sichuan seemed an impregnable fortress—impervious to all incursions from the outside world, much less ones that could seriously threaten its wild lands. Today, only the upper reaches of the region are still largely untouched. The the broad eastern periphery of the wilderness has not been so fortunate. It already shows signs of wear and tear attributable to its proximity to population centers.

If the fringes of western Sichuan do not survive, much stands to be lost. Eventually, even the loftiest strongholds—places such as Gongga Shan and the Kangba Plateau—could begin to show the effects. For now, western Sichuan is gloriously untamed, still one of the wildest places on earth. On the eve of a new century and millennium, one hopes that there will never be a cause to lament that it has become something less.

The threatening snout of a gharial eyeing the world above water belies the fish-eater's shy disposition.

*M*Y FIRST VISIT TO THIS FORMER HUNTING preserve of the maharajas was in 1987. Sitting in the foothills of the Himalayas in southern Nepal, Royal Chitwan National Park is a magnificent sanctuary of rivers, grasslands and thick forests that harbor an extraordinary range of wildlife—including marsh, mugger and gharial crocodiles, six or seven types of deer, langur monkeys, leopards, Indian elephants, Bengal tigers and endangered Indian rhinos.

I was fortunate enough to join in the search for a tiger that had been prowling the outskirts of a village near the southern boundary of the park. There was reason for concern: Chitwan tigers kill on average one villager each year. Once found and fitted with a radio collar, the tiger could be monitored. If its terrain fell near the village, the tiger would be relocated to a remote corner of the park.

Before the search began, our hunting party underwent a purification ritual. Amid chanting and the burning of incense in a clearing in the woods, a local priest cut the throats of several chickens and sprinkled their blood on the ground. Next, he sacrificed a goat, mixing its blood with red dyes and smearing the mixture on our foreheads. Later that night we feasted on the meat.

The next morning we set off on elephants into the park. Wading through meadows of ten-foot-high elephant grass, we came upon rhinos wallowing in small ponds on a floodplain. They trotted out of the water, snorted and honked, then stomped their feet and charged the ele-

phants, pulling up just short. I was glad to be on the back of an elephant, well beyond reach of their horns. Within an hour we came to the site where a water-buffalo calf had been set out the night before as bait for the tiger. The bait was gone, and our search was on.

Once the route taken by the tiger had been determined, a wide band of white cloth about a thousand yards long was strung through the woods. The strategy, borrowed from the maharajas, was to create a visual barrier that would direct the tiger along a narrowing path to a known end point. There, on a platform built in the trees, a shooter who was armed with a tranquilizer gun would be waiting.

Shaded from the sun by black umbrellas, elephant-riding drivers lined up behind beaters, who yelled as loudly as possible and banged on tin pots and other noisemakers. Moving abreast through the tall grass, we headed for the mouth of our funnel-shaped course. Forty-five minutes later, not a blade of grass had moved in the woods ahead of us. I was certain that there had been a mistake, that no tiger had been trapped. But I was wrong.

Like a one-horned tank, a rhino burst into the open and out the end of the funnel, tearing a gaping hole in the cloth barrier. Following it was the tiger, a young female about three-quarters grown. The canny tigress—apparently she had used the rhino as a decoy—was an easy tar-

A tangled patchwork of rivers, grasslands
and forests, Royal Chitwan blankets an
area of 360 square miles at the foot of the
Himalayas in southern Nepal.

get to dart; fearing nothing from above, she never looked
up. After a hasty fitting with a radio collar, she was given
an antidote and released to begin supplying data on the
scope of her hunting grounds.

This story exemplifies the ongoing struggle by park
officials to balance the often-conflicting needs of the local
residents and the wildlife. The challenge confronting
Royal Chitwan—and most other parks throughout the
developing world—is to somehow distribute more of
the rewards for protecting wilderness to the people who live on its frontiers.

—JF

ROYAL CHITWAN

BY DOUGLAS H. CHADWICK

Stretched out beneath a gentle blanket of mist, the countryside seems slow to awaken. Bird songs from the forest are few and faint, and even the voice of the nearby river is barely a whisper.

A faint rustling in the vegetation induces a shudder—the source of the noise is fairly close at hand. But the elephant grass along the floodplain is thick as cane and, at 15 feet tall, more than high enough to guard its secrets. Judging from the number of trampled paths and droppings, these stalks may be hiding quite a few rhinoceroses. Worse still, the cool, gray hours of the morning are a perfect time for a Bengal tiger to be on the prowl. The pugmarks along the river's shore may have been fresher than they seemed.

Royal Chitwan National Park, the vine-knit wilderness stronghold near Nepal's southern border, is well named: Chitwan is said to mean "heart of the jungle." And in terms of the jungle balance of power, an unarmed human, easily unnerved by sudden noises, is indeed a poor match for many of the possible causes.

Straining ears hear mostly the sound of racing blood. Breathing grows shallow, until a furred body flashes into view. Ah! It is only a little muntjac, an exotic barking deer with small tusks to match its antlers. Its coat glistening with dew, the muntjac glances about, then vanishes into the elephant grass to continue the search for sprouts. Farther on, the grasses part to reveal a much larger deer that raises its head from the edge of a marsh. The long sweep of antlers identifies it as a male sambar, close kin to the European red deer and the North American elk.

From the forest comes a sudden chorus of screams. Peacocks, the great, glittering fowl so common along the woodlands' edge, no longer startle with their piercing calls. Still, their cries often herald the passing of other beasts, and by now there is the gnawing feeling that the time has come to abandon this thicket.

The loop back to the river is quick; an open beach becomes an invitation to rest and watch the mist slowly dissipate. Marsh and mugger crocodiles waddle ashore to bask in the first weak rays of sunlight. A very different-looking crocodile hauls itself out onto a sandbar in the river's center. It is a gharial, a shy creature identifiable by its long, narrow snout and needle-like teeth. Stretching nearly 20 feet from snout to tail tip, this one looks like a beached dragon.

As the visibility improves, huge bombax trees take shape on the far bank and giant hornbills can be seen flying among them. The sound of the birds' wings as they labor through the air brings to mind a local legend. These heavy fowl are said to be born in the tops of the very tallest trees and to gradually lose altitude throughout the remainder of their days.

Finally, the last of the fog evaporates, and the peacock-blue sky holds only a single

Within view of the bleary Himalayas, yet somehow part of an altogether different world, the Narayani River snakes through Royal Chitwan National Park.

Rays of sun piercing the forest canopy warm the ground for a basking lizard.

bank of clouds in the distance. But it is one last trick of the eye. For these are not clouds, but mountains—impossible, ice-crowned towers of stone projecting skyward 25,000 feet and more. They are the Himalayas, an abode of yaks and snow leopards, and gods beyond counting. And they are no more than 100 miles from this place where crocodiles sleep in the sun.

Perhaps only the gods could fully explain how this part of the world came to hold such spectacular variety. Geologists speak of a monumental collision between the once separate Indian subcontinent and the endless landmass of Asia, an impact that thrust the Himalayas into the stratosphere. The same pressures are said to have created two parallel folds to the south: the Mahabharat Range and the more modest Siwalik Hills, which rise to somewhere between 2,500 and 5,000 feet before giving way to the vast, level plain of the Ganges River in northern India.

The steamy valleys that lie between the Mahabharats and Siwalik Hills form Nepal's belt of tropical lowlands, known as the Terai. For centuries the Terai was inhabited by only a few scattered fishing communities and tribes of subsistence farmers. The jungles were nearly impenetrable—in part because they harbored so much dangerous wildlife. Deadliest of all were not the king cobras, the sloth bears or even the big, hungry cats. That honor fell to the humble mosquito, which

Locked in the clockwise stranglehold of a climbing vine, a sal tree seems threatened with being uprooted.

A pit viper, which uses heat sensors below its nostrils to detect warm-blooded prey, coils into a knot to rest.

carried a virulent strain of malaria. The Terai thus helped insulate Nepal from the outside world and allowed the unique Himalayan culture to flourish, with its center in the fabled Kathmandu.

When the Ranas usurped power in the kingdom in 1846, they chose the Chitwan region of the Terai as their exclusive hunting reserve. They saw to it that the wildlife was well protected—from the commoners, at least. Every so often the nobles themselves would invade en masse. The lords, draped in silk and spangled with jewels, would be attended by servants on their elephants, while hundreds of men beat the bush in their path. One royal hunt in the winter of 1938 and 1939 claimed 15 bears, 38 rhinos, 27 leopards and 120 tigers. As long as the habitat stayed intact, however, the wildlife was able to recover.

The game reserve came to an end in 1950 along with the Ranas' power. In the years that followed, an intensive chemical spraying program eradicated malaria in the lowlands. The plan was to open the Terai to settlers, and the scheme worked well, although it had some unfortunate consequences. Land-hungry people spilled down from the hills like a monsoon flood. Almost overnight, the Terai became Nepal's most heavily populated region, and fields under cultivation were hard up against the remaining forest lands.

Of the animal species that suffered as a result, the Indian one-horned rhinoceros was one of the hardest hit. While farmers claimed more and more of the rhinoceroses' habitat in the fertile floodplains, poachers were taking increasing numbers of the animals purely for the sake of their horns, which were prized for ceremonial and medicinal uses. By 1950, the only large concentration of rhinoceroses left on the subcontinent were the 1,000 or so in and around Chitwan. Scarcely a hundred of those remained a decade later. In 1962 the king of Nepal set aside 210 square miles along the confluence of the Narayani, Rapti and Reu Rivers and in adjoining areas of the Siwalik Hills as a rhinoceros sanctuary. In 1973 the reserve was declared a national park. The encroachment on Chitwan's undeveloped lands finally came to an end. Nothing dampened the price of rhinoceros horn, however, and the illegal killings continued until an army unit took up residence in the park.

Today, Chitwan is the home of some 400 Indian one-horned rhinoceroses, a quarter of the animals still in existence. The population has been tapped to stock another reserve located in Nepal.

Probably the best way to observe the ancient, armored beasts is from the vantage familiar to the old Rana nobles: seated in a howdah on the back of an elephant, with a mahout astride the neck to pilot the giant. Visibility is not obstructed by the elephant grass, and ambling right up to a rhinoceros is possible. The temperamental beasts are nev-

Wading the waters along a riverbank, a curious-looking Bengal tiger steadies its gaze and cocks its ears toward the source of its interest.

Paw prints along a mucky shoreline betray the stealthy passage of a great cat.

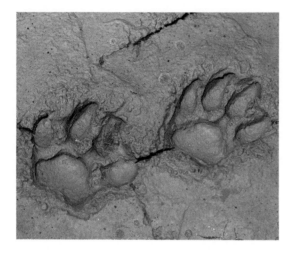

er pleased to have company, but even those with the shortest fuses know better than to charge a fully grown elephant.

Researchers often travel by this means when they study the park's tigers, but not every feline is suitably intimidated. A cornered cat once landed on an elephant's forehead with its first leap and with its next was swatting at the horrified riders.

With the exception of humans, tigers have always been the main predator of the Asian elephant; they are more than willing to attack the young of a herd whenever the opportunity arises. Wild elephants were common in the Terai until farms hemmed in the region. The odd herd still shows up now and then, having made its way along the Siwalik Hills from the fragments of wildland left in India.

Like rhinoceroses, gharial crocodiles came perilously close to extinction in recent

decades. Changes to the habitat robbed them of their homes and poachers coveted their skins. Once again, Chitwan served as a haven for the largest single group of survivors. In addition to providing them refuge along the park's rivers, officials built a hatchery and successfully reared young gharials for return to the wild.

While much of Chitwan's wealth of life is concentrated in the floodplains, still other riches dwell half-hidden among the shadows of the woodlands. Three-quarters of the park is cloaked in monsoon forest. Drenched by downpours from June through September, the ground nevertheless becomes very dry over the months that follow, and wildfires periodically sweep the forest floor. The trees that can withstand such extremes are species such as sal, its hardwood resistant to rot and flames alike, and saz, or *Terminalia*, which has a bark as tough as crocodile skin. These are merely the scaffolding, however, upon which the true jungle climbs. Strangler figs

wrap around the tree trunks, while mosses and ferns cling to the limbs. Vines and creepers web the branches, carrying nutrients to bright sprays of flowers high in the canopy. Pale orchids unfold from debris caught in crevices below. So profuse is the growth that the very air seems to be crisscrossed by tendrils of scent.

On the forest floor, herds of gaur graze close together. Sometimes called Indian bison, they are the region's most massive cloven-hooved creatures, growing up to seven feet tall at the shoulder. Bluish-black in color, they have the look of condensed twilight. But they make no secret of their presence, grunting and snorting as they scratch against tree trunks and wallow in the dirt to coat their hides against insects.

Chital, or axis deer, slip past seedlings and clumps of bamboo in more open sections of the understory. Their white-spotted coats blend with the dappled light that penetrates the canopy, giving them a special aura

Spotted deer known as chital graze the grassy Terai.

A dour-looking Indian one-horned rhinoceros feeds on elephant grasses.

of softness and grace. Even so, there is always an ear cocked, a foot halting in mid-stride. When the deer startle, the cause may be nothing more than langur monkeys or rhesus macaques crashing through the branches overhead. Yet there is always the threat of leopards in these trees. The region is also home to Indian pythons, hyenas and the occasional pack of dholes, also known as Indian wild dogs.

The longest claws in the forest belong to the sloth bears. Local villagers repeat frightening tales of how these fierce creatures go for the face when attacking. In truth, however, the bears are far more likely to flee at the sight of a human. They use their mighty claws primarily to tear open the tall earthen mounds that rise from the forest floor. This done, the bears can then lick up the termites that are a staple of their diet.

For their part, the termites far outnumber all of the mammals in the park. And these lowly insects play a vital ecological role, processing and recycling tremendous quantities of vegetation.

Chitwan is not just the wild reserve of the long-fanged and the sharp of claw; it teems with creatures of all kinds. Indeed, the very presence of large, powerful species is the sure sign of a thriving, well-balanced community of animals with a diverse array of smaller life forms.

The park has already played a crucial role in the survival of threatened species. But there are serious questions about whether or not it can continue to be such an effective preserve of wildness. Rhinoceroses can exist at high densities within a fairly limited area because they usually do not range very far. Tigers, on the other hand, can require hundreds of square miles to thrive. Unless widely dispersed, they quickly deplete their food supply. By way of example, several hundred chital are needed to produce enough of their kind each year to feed a single Bengal tiger. The original park contained insufficient space for more than two or three dozen of

By day fruit bats hang upside-down in trees, their wings slung from branches like hammocks.

Perched on a carcass, an Indian white-backed vulture spreads its wings as if addressing the guests at a banquet.

the striped cats. However, such a small, isolated population would be highly vulnerable to disease, drought and the consequences of inbreeding. The only viable option was to expand the boundaries of the park. And, in 1979, the government of Nepal saw fit to do exactly that—nearly doubling the size of the territory to 360 square miles.

Further expansion is unlikely, however, and the challenge today is to integrate the wild realm of Chitwan with the ever more crowded human communities that surround it. This is being attempted in a variety of ways. An interesting example is the compensation made to neighboring farmers whose crops are damaged by animals straying from the park—rhinoceroses being the worst offenders. The park contains the only major stands of elephant grass left in the region and, from time to time, villagers are allowed to harvest the growth for fodder, roof thatching and other traditional uses. Future goals are to share more of the income generated by tourism with the neighboring population and to develop corridors of habitat that would link the region with other wilderness reserves.

Such concerns, obviously, are removed from everyday life in Chitwan. Afternoon's heat and musky odors linger in the gather-

A displaying peacock fans the iridescent plumes of its tail.

ing gloom of the forest as evening approaches. The thick air fills with an insect chorus that pulses and rings like rubbed glass. Fruit bats known as flying foxes dart among the trees, and wild boars snuffle in the undergrowth. Sunset is the time to return to the open riverside and watch the Himalayas catch fire. Long after dusk arrives, the peaks are still alive, as if filled to the brim with glowing embers.

A splash breaks the reverie. Crocodile? Probably, but the light has grown too dim to be sure. The sound could also have been made by a Gangetic dolphin, another species whose tenuous existence has been given a boost by Chitwan. A second splash—this one not as loud as the first. Perhaps it marks the passage of a smooth-coated otter. For all the dark currents reveal, however, it may as well have been the surfacing of a river god.

Out of the ill-lit expanse of tall grass that sweeps from the trees toward shore comes a scratchy-throated cough: unmistakably that of a cat. This is an unequivocal signal for the listener to depart. From the beating heart of the jungle has come another reminder that humans do not prevail everywhere—not yet. Chitwan still exists on its own terms, like the indomitable mountains now turning the color of moonlight, so high and yet so near.

Conspicuous even in a rare quiet moment, a roosting hornbill peers out past its long, ridge-casqued bill.

*I*N 1987 I TRAVELED WITH A FILM CREW INTO SOME of the wilder reaches of Sumatra, a huge island in the archipelago of Indonesia. The purpose of our expedition was to shoot footage of the orangutan, a shy, long-limbed primate that dwells in the tropical rain forest. The orangutan—a name meaning "man of the forest"—has few wildlife enemies. Like all the great apes, however, the species is endangered. Humans are the principal threat, with loggers destroying the habitat and poachers killing mothers to sell their infants as pets.

In Sumatra's northern province of Aceh, the Indonesian government has established Gunung Leuser National Park, a vast tract of remote jungle surrounding the more than 10,000-foot-high summit for which the reserve is named. This mountain—the translation of "gunung"—is the tallest peak of the Bukit Barisan. We were headed for the Bohorok Orangutan Rehabilitation Station on the eastern edge of the park where orphaned apes are readied for life in the wilderness.

To reach the station, we rafted for seven thrilling days along the Alas River. We crashed through rock-studded rapids and floated by waterfalls tumbling crystal-clear from high overhead. The air was rife with sounds of the jungle, which shelters such wildlife as Sumatran elephants, tigers and rhinos, leopards, gibbons and their close cousins, the siamangs. This region supports a greater variety of plants than virtually any other place in the world. It even has the rare Rafflesia arnoldii, which unfurls blooms a full three feet wide. As we navigated the river, we passed through brilliant clouds of butterflies.

We left the Alas to trek east along forest trails to the Bohorok River. There, a hand-operated ferry was used to bring us across the swift-flowing waters. We then followed a steep, winding path deep into the wilderness.

At the station, rangers set out food twice daily for the orangutans undergoing rehabilitation, luring them out of the forest. We were obliged to keep at a distance because of the threat of infection. A human with a minor respiratory ailment could easily start a contagion that might wipe out the local ape population.

Standing off to one side, we watched in fascination as the orangutans fed and swung by their long arms through the trees. Some of them deftly drank milk from cups, a practice learned in captivity. The youngest rehabilitant was two years old; the oldest was nine.

Orangutans, along with gorillas and chimpanzees, are mankind's closest living relatives and the next most intelligent species. Unlike their other primate kin, adult orangutans are essentially solitary beings. They are gentle, unaggressive creatures and have never been observed to kill. By day a male may roam as much as one and a half miles in search of fruit in the trees. Typically, he will at least once emit a bellowing call to warn off other males and alert females of his availability. Females are usually accompanied by one or two dependent offspring. Every morning they abandon the nests that they made in the trees the night before and move on.

A favorite food of orangutans is the durian, a thorny-husked, melon-size fruit that smells like untreated sewage. If the odor can be ignored, the fruit tastes like an avocado spiked with almond liqueur. Durians can be smelled a mile away and we followed their scent in hopes of seeing orangutans in the wild. Our noses led us to plenty of durians, but we never spotted an ape. We hiked as far up as 7,000 feet, but were rewarded with merely the unforgettable bellowing of male orangutans off in the distance.

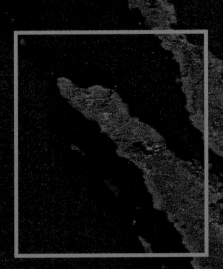

Situated on the island of Sumatra,
Indonesia's Gunung Leuser National
Park encompasses 3,120 square miles
of jungle and one the world's richest
assortments of animals and plants.

However, we came across tracks of a Sumatran tiger
and had a close encounter with a Burmese python. From
afar, we saw Sumatran elephants and, at one point, we
found a pond that had been recently vacated by a
Sumatran rhino. We considered ourselves extremely fortunate to get even this close to one of maybe a hundred of
this species still alive.

Although orangutans are being returned to the wild,
they still face extinction without protection of the rain
forest—their only natural habitat. Large areas of forest
beyond the park have been destroyed by logging. And
slash-and-burn agriculture encroaches on the forest even
within the park.

Thankfully, there are efforts being made to preserve
what remains of the habitat for orangutans—and the
other unique species of the region. I left Sumatra taking
warm memories and a glimmer of hope that maybe, just
maybe, the wildlife of the area might survive to touch the
human heart and conscience forever.

—JF

GUNUNG LEUSER

BY GREG STOTT

From deep within the jungle comes a loud, shuddering groan. Gradually building in volume, it climaxes in a robust roar that lasts fully a minute and can be heard nearly a mile away.

The source of the bellowing is a full-grown male orangutan. His reddish-gold fur glints among the lower branches of a vine-snarled tree that pokes upward into a canopy of green 170 feet above the ground. Plucking a ripe durian, he methodically peels off the hard, prickly rind and eats the fruit. Satisfied, he descends to the ground and lumbers on into the dense tangle of rain forest that is one of the last remaining refuges of his species.

In his retreat, the orangutan brushes against a *Rafflesia arnoldii,* the world's largest flower. Foul smelling but spectacular, its brilliant brick-red and white-speckled blossom weighs some 15 pounds and opens a yard in diameter. Insects lured by the rancid scent swarm over the flower. The plant is a parasite without roots or green photosynthetic tissues; it grows from wild grapevines in a few patches of jungle in the region.

Like the orangutan, the *Rafflesia arnoldii* is one of the many intriguing emblems of Indonesia's Gunung Leuser National Park—a rolling, rain-soaked reserve that drapes the northern Bukit Barisan, Sumatra's thousand-mile-long "parade of mountains." From species-rich lowland jungles, the park rises up through mossy, river-laced forests to scrub peaks as high as 11,400 feet.

After falling ten times steeper than the Colorado River through the Grand Canyon, the Alas River slows through the forested foothills of Gunung Leuser National Park on its way to the Indian Ocean.

This extraordinary place is blessed with flora and fauna that make it one of the most opulent natural sanctuaries in the world. It is an Eden in a precarious balance, however, and upon its future hinge the survival of species such as the *Rafflesia arnoldii* and creatures such as the orangutan, the Sumatran tiger and the Sumatran rhinoceros.

In the scheme of national parks worldwide, the 3,120-square-mile Gunung Leuser ranks as one of the largest; it is roughly equivalent in size to the island of Puerto Rico. The park is a relatively recent creation, conceived in the 1970s and born in 1980 by Indonesia's Ministry of Agriculture with the midwifery of the World Wildlife Fund. Like many others of its kind, the park was the off-spring of ominous scientific forecasts on the integrity of wilderness regions and of political recognition of the need for safeguards.

The story is sadly familiar. The countryside had flourished down through the centuries, but unchecked exploitation of the land in recent years exacted a severe toll on the wildlife. Logging devoured large tracts of virgin rain forest. And plantation-style farming became the norm, consuming huge portions of terrain.

Hunters were equally insensitive to the rhythms of a delicately tuned ecosystem. Poachers slaughtered the rhinoceroses for their horns and wholesaled them to dealers in Asia. There, the keratin was ground to a powder and sold as an aphrodisiac.

Sumatran tigers fell victim to a similar legend—their whiskers were purported to bestow sexual prowess. The lithe, handsome cats were also pursued for their luxuriant skins and in retribution for supposed transgressions in killing cattle or humans. Today, fewer than 90 Sumatran tigers are estimated to remain.

The orangutan and Malay sun bear have suffered too, again for human whimsy. Sadly, a common practice was to shoot the mother apes and bears so that the babies could be more easily obtained for the pet trade. As recently as the 1960s, hundreds of orphaned young were being sold every year in the villages and port towns of Sumatra.

Even fish became valuable chattel. Pet store bounty hunters have scoured Sumatra's northern rivers for the golden arowana, a dragonfish that is the world's most expensive aquarium species.

On an island where a burgeoning human population—currently numbering about 40 million—is desperate for agricultural land, such mercenary pastimes and black markets have proven to be extremely hard to discourage. But with the founding of Gunung Leuser National Park and the hiring of park wardens, there is now hope that some of Sumatra's unique wildlife can endure in unspoiled surroundings.

Indonesia ranks today as the world's top exporter of tropical hardwoods. The original forests that once covered all of Sumatra have been reduced by close to 80 percent. Although still lush, with the exception of Gunung Leuser, the island bears little resemblance to the one encountered long ago by Marco Polo.

The monsoon season, scourge of ancient mariners, compelled the intrepid Venetian explorer and trader to land at Sumatra in

ABOVE, LEFT: *A squawking macaque flashes its teeth in fury.* ABOVE: *On branch-clinging arms, a siamang swoops through the forest.*

A marble-eyed binturong glares from the jungle floor.

1292. After lingering five months on the island, he returned home with accounts of poison arrows, cannibalism and monstrous flowers that fascinated medieval Europe. In his journal, *The Travels of Marco Polo,* he also reported on an unusual-looking unicorn— no doubt a Sumatran rhinoceros. Marco Polo wrote as well of "men with tails, a span in length, like those of a dog, but not covered with hair." Tales of a Sumatran ape-man have persisted ever since.

According to the Kubu, Sumatra's last truly nomadic people, this singular creature walks with backward-pointing feet to confuse his pursuers. The 1891 discovery of skeletal remains of Java man, an extinct race of hominid, encouraged speculation that perhaps some type of man-ape species did in fact exist in remote parts of the jungle. Dutch settlers in Sumatra embraced the legend well into the 1900s with reported sightings of large, mysterious creatures that had human-like features.

Several explanations have been offered. One theory postulates that the mystery primate is actually the Malay sun bear, which can reach four feet in height and will stand, but not walk, on its two hind legs. Another hypothesis puts forward the notion that the creature is probably an oversized siamang, a small ape that is the only indigenous primate to walk on its hind legs. Contrary to the descriptions of Marco Polo, however, the siamang has no tail.

The sixth largest island in the world, Sumatra lies directly on important equatorial travel routes and has witnessed the arrival of many seafarers since the days of Marco Polo. The island's history is long on foreigners who came to set up trading posts or to conquer and rule. Since the 16th century, the land has been either occupied or claimed by

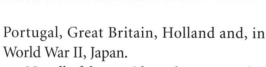

A scruffy-looking orangutan lurches down from a tree.

Nibbling quietly on foliage, a female orangutan appears to be savoring her greens.

Portugal, Great Britain, Holland and, in World War II, Japan.

Not all of the outsiders who came to this wilderness, however, were mere merchants or colonizers. Sir Thomas Stamford Raffles, a British colonial administrator, fell under the spell of the rich botanical treasures in the region. He and naturalist Joseph Arnold are credited with official discovery in the early 1800s of the plant that bears their latinized names: *Rafflesia arnoldii.*

The botanical find was recorded a little more than 130 years before sovereignty was finally returned to the people of Indonesia in 1949. Stability was longer in coming to the land, however, arriving only after bitter civil

wars among the country's many ethnic communities. When peace was attained in the staunchly Muslim nation, attention turned to the development of industry and the struggle for economic growth.

Smoke-belching oil and gas refineries are among the visible signs of this push for a modern industrial economy. Another hallmark is the Trans-Sumatran Highway, a 1,500-mile-long stretch of blacktop that spans the island. Passing large palm oil plantations, aging rubber estates and broad rice fields, this highway climbs into the Bukit Barisan and bisects Gunung Leuser National Park before descending into the central valley of the Alas River. While it greatly eases trans-

portation across the island, the road also constitutes a major barrier to the movements of many species of wildlife. And by attracting settlers who wish to carve out farms along its forested perimeter, the highway carries the risk of encouraging still further encroachment on the wilderness.

Yet the damp, leech-riddled jungle surrounding Gunung Leuser is itself a rather formidable barrier—enough so in some instances to put a damper on development schemes. Moreover, what is inhospitable to humans is, in this case, most remarkably amenable to other forms of life. Scientists believe that this rain forest is home to some 105 types of mammals, 76 kinds of reptiles, 18 varieties of amphibians and more than 313 species of birds.

For some of this population, however, the future is highly uncertain. Sumatran rhinoceroses, for example, now number no more than 100 and possibly fewer than 50. Readily identified by their long, primordial snouts with two small horns, these diffident beasts are small for their species, weighing only about 2,000 pounds. That is roughly half the bulk of an Indian rhinoceros. The hinterlands of Gunung Leuser are the last wilderness asylum in the world for this vanishing breed. Only extremely rarely nowadays, one of the creatures will be spotted browsing contentedly on leaves and twigs in

a marsh or poking about on a forested hill close to water.

Although utterly unique, the Sumatran rhinoceros does have a namesake in the rhinoceros hornbill. This boisterous bird stands about two or three feet in height, and has a huge beak crowned by a protruding, casque-like growth that resembles the horn of a rhinoceros. As dawn steals slowly through the jungle, the whistling, cackling, grunting and wing-flapping of the colorful hornbill can be heard above the many other sounds of animals coming to life—earning the bird a reputation as the "clamor and glamour" fowl of the Sumatran forest.

The title is one that several other birds seem to vie for. Perhaps the most pompous-looking competitor is the Argus pheasant, which takes full advantage of its grandiose tail feathers as it puffs itself out to a length of almost six feet and shrieks an imperial "ku-ow." Not to be outdone, the long-tailed helmeted hornbill delivers a fast-tempoed "hoop-hoop-hoop," and an eared nightjar skims the tall trees, whistling final renditions of its "tok-tedau" before going into hiding for the day.

Another sound of greeting in the jungle is the ear-splitting trumpeting of the mighty Sumatran elephant. The largest beast of the region, this creature once paraded freely throughout much of Indonesia. Sadly, its

FAR LEFT: *The placid-looking imperial pigeon can distend its beak to swallow fruit whole.* NEAR LEFT: *The fairy bluebird whistles a song as iridescent as its plumage.*

numbers in Sumatra have dwindled to no more than several hundred. Surviving members of the entire species in all of Asia are estimated to be in the neighborhood of 2,000, with possibly as many as 300 of these the Sumatran elephants that live in the shadows of Gunung Leuser.

As the chorus of elephant trumpets has diminished, the calls of other mammals have become more pronounced. Among the most ubiquitous voices are those of the gibbons, which hold forth from high in the branches of trees. The melancholy whoops and plaintive wails of these primates seem to hang in the musty air like a mournful lament.

None can hold a candle, however, to the male orangutans. The commanding calls of these long-armed apes often seem to drown out all other sound. And as strident as the creatures are to the ear, they are as equally impressive to the eye.

A research site where orangutans can be observed is located at Bukit Lawang, a few hours by road west of Medan, the bustling capital of northern Sumatra. There, at the Bohorok Orangutan Rehabilitation Station, young orangutans who have been left homeless by logging or orphaned by poachers are trained to survive in the wild.

The undertaking is perhaps key to the survival of the species. As recently as 1990, the International Primate Protection League reported that more than 1,000 orangutans had been smuggled out of the wilderness and

With its gaudy train of feathers, the Argus pheasant somehow resembles a fanciful child dressed up in its mother's clothing.

NEAR RIGHT: *Cycles of cannibalism by the flour beetle improve the species' fertility.*
FAR RIGHT: *A forest spider spins a web of glistening silk to capture insects.*

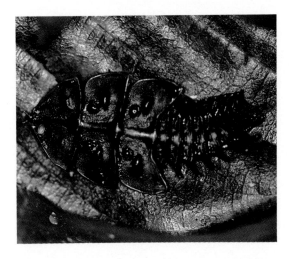 

shipped to Taiwan aboard fishing boats. On their arrival, they would have been purchased for their meat or for use in traditional herbal medicines.

Since the opening of the rehabilitation station by two Swiss scientists in 1973, more than 150 young apes have been successfully weaned from human care and returned to the rain forest for life on their own. This is, perhaps, a modest achievement when viewed against the large numbers of animals removed, but it is also a hard-won victory and a positive step toward preserving the natural character of the region.

Arguably the most pristine wilderness in all of Sumatra, the interior north of Gunung Leuser is gloriously untamed and still largely unexplored. From its source in the highlands of Aceh, the Alas River tumbles to the east, in places turning to foamy rapids that blast through steep limestone gorges. The lush, vine-draped rain forest along the shores is woven so tightly that the river seems to flow between solid walls of green. Somehow penetrating the muting foliage, a cacophony of jungle sounds escapes to mix with the hissing music of the waters.

At a quiet bend in the river, a diving grasshopper rises briefly to the surface. A few moments later, a chirping cricket that brandishes eight-inch antennae appears at the mouth of a small cave by the shoreline.

Moving down its course, the Alas passes an opening in the forest. The broken branches and torn saplings are the work of a herd of nearly 40 elephants, which are busily munching on foliage and grasses. They have voracious appetites. To maintain the enormous bulk of their four- to five-ton bodies, they must each consume several hundred pounds of food every day. Elephants also drink a quota of about 25 gallons of water a day, a thirst that brings them often to the riverbank. Using their trunks as siphons, they guzzle their fill, making an exhilarating racket in the process.

Off to one side of the clearing, two bulls spar trunk-to-trunk in a kind of mock combat. The older male is about 30 years of age. If he lives a full life, he will roam the herd's ancient migration routes for perhaps another three decades.

But with the advantages that humans wield in competing for the resources of the land, neither the fate of the bull nor the future of the herd is assured. Fortunately, Gunung Leuser National Park provides a secure wilderness sanctuary, a protected habitat where endangered species such as the elephants, rhinoceroses and tigers have at least a fighting chance to survive, perhaps even to flourish.

There are no guarantees however. People will need to continue to respect the entitlement of wildlife to a portion of the land. And the pressures to encroach on the wilderness areas remaining can only be expected to grow more intense.

By breaking down the dead matter of a fallen log, fungi benefit the forest ecosystem.

The brilliant, yard-wide bloom of a rare Rafflesia arnoldii *unfolds in full, malodorous splendor.*

A giant tree fern opens like an umbrella above the jungle.

Conflicting political claims seem virtually inevitable; there will be a steady stream of difficult trade-offs confronting government decision-makers. Indonesia, with nearly 200 million people, is currently one of the most populous nations in the world. The Alas Valley alone is already home to more than 100,000 settlers. Skyrocketing social costs—for education, in particular—underscore the temptation to yield to industries such as logging, mining and rubber that generate the tax dollars.

The challenge of the future for Gunung Leuser National Park will be to somehow reconcile the competing needs of wildlife and people in a way that benefits both. If that can be done, one of the wildest places on earth will have the opportunity to endure.

PHOTO CREDITS

Rainbow Valley, Australia, by Gerry Ellis; bison by Wolfgang Kaehler; red-footed booby by Wolfgang Kaehler; red-eyed leaf frog by Stephen Dalton; checkerboard wrasse and grouper by Jeff Rotman; great gray kangaroo by Gerry Ellis; red lechwe by Tim Liversedge. 18 Ian Gittler. BROOKS RANGE: 20,21 Kim Heacox; 24 Kim Heacox; 26,27 Michio Hoshino/Minden Pictures; 27 (right) Kim Heacox; 28 (lower left) Kim Heacox; 28,29 (upper) Tom Bean; 28,29 (lower) Kim Heacox; 30 Robert Winslow/Tom Stack & Associates; 31 Jeff Foott/Tom Stack & Associates; 32,33 Steve Kaufman/Natural Selection; 34 (left) Kim Heacox; 34,35 (upper) Kim Heacox; 34,35 (lower) Tom Bean; 35 (right) Kim Heacox; 36 Kim Heacox; 37 Kim Heacox. RORAIMA: 38,39 Jay Dickman; 42 Thomas C. Boyden; 44,45 (both) Jay Dickman; 46,47 (both) Jay Dickman; 48,49 (both) Jay Dickman; 50 (upper left, lower) Thomas C. Boyden; 50 (upper right) Jay Dickman; 51 Thomas C. Boyden; 52, 53 Jay Dickman; 54 (upper left) Thomas C. Boyden; 54 (lower) Jay Dickman; 54,55 Thomas C. Boyden. TORRES DEL PAINE: 56,57 Freeman Patterson/Masterfile; 60 Wolfgang Kaehler; 62,63 (all) Wolfgang Kaehler; 64,65 (both) Wolfgang Kaehler; 66,67 (all) Wolfgang Kaehler; 68,69 Wolfgang Kaehler; 70 (upper) Wolfgang Kaehler; 70, 71 (lower) Freeman Patterson/Masterfile; 71 (upper left, upper right) Wolfgang Kaehler; 72 Wolfgang Kaehler; 73 Joe McDonald/Animals Animals; 74,75 Wolfgang Kaehler. ANTARCTIC PENINSULA: 76,77 Frans Lanting/Minden Pictures; 80 Wolfgang Kaehler; 82,83 Wolfgang Kaehler; 84,85 Wolfgang Kaehler; 85 (right) William Curtsinger/Photo Researchers; 86,87 Wofgang Kaehler; 88,89 (all) Wolfgang Kaehler; 90,91 (all) Wolfgang Kaehler; 92 (left) Peter Johnson/NHPA; 92,93 Wolfgang Kaehler. MOUNTAINS OF THE MOON: 94,95 Boyd Norton; 98 Boyd Norton; 100 (upper) Gerry Ellis; 100 (lower) Heather Angel; 101 Heather Angel; 102,103 (both) Gerry Ellis; 104 Boyd Norton; 105 (left, lower right) Boyd Norton; 105 (upper right) Dianne Blell; 106,107 Gerry Ellis; 108 (upper left, lower left) Gerry Ellis; 108,109 Boyd Norton; 109 (upper right) Heather Angel; 109 (lower right) Gerry Ellis; 110,111 (both) Heather Angel. OKAVANGO DELTA: 112,113 Beverly Joubert/ABPL; 116 George Calef/Masterfile; 118 (left) George Calef/Masterfile; 118,119 Gregory D. Dimijian/Photo Researchers; 120 (upper left) George Calef/Masterfile; 120 (lower left) Frans Lanting/Minden Pictures; 120,121 Frans Lanting/Minden Pictures; 121 (lower) Daryl Balfour/ABPL; 122,123 Frans Lanting/Minden Pictures; 124,125 Frans Lanting/Minden Pictures; 126 (lower) Gregory Dimijian/Photo Researchers; 126,127 Frans Lanting/Minden Pictures; 128,129 Frans Lanting/Minden Pictures; 129 (upper right) Frans Lanting/Minden Pictures; 129 (middle) George Calef/Masterfile; 129 (lower left) Gregory G. Dimijian/Photo Researchers; 130,131 George Calef/Masterfile. SKELETON COAST: 132,133 Anthony Bannister/ABPL; 136 Anthony Bannister/ABPL; 138 (lower) Anthony Bannister/ABPL; 138,139 Jim Brandenberg/Minden Pictures; 139 (lower) Anthony Bannister/ABPL; 140 Jim Brandenberg/Minden Pictures; 141 (both) Anthony Bannister/ABPL; 142 (left, upper right) Diane Blell; 142 (lower right) Gavin Thomson/ABPL; 142,143 Diane Blell; 144,145 Jim Brandenberg/Minden Pictures; 146 (upper left, upper right) Dr. J.R. Henschel/ABPL; 146,147 Gavin Thomson/ABPL; 147 (upper left, upper right) Anthony Bannister/ABPL; 148 Gavin Thomson/ABPL; 149 Diane Blell. LAKE BAIKAL: 150,151 Boyd Norton; 154 Boyd Norton; 156,157 Boyd Norton; 158 (upper) Rick Sammon; 158,159 Boyd Norton; 159 (both) Rick Sammon; 160,161 Boyd Norton; 162 Boyd Norton; 163 (left) Maresa Pryor/Animals Animals; 163 (right) Eric A. Soder/Tom Stack & Associates; 164,165 (both) Art Wolfe; 166,167 (both) Boyd Norton. WESTERN SICHUAN: 168,169 Pat Morrow; 172 Pat Morrow; 174 Pat Morrow; 175 Heather Angel; 176 (lower) Heather Angel; 176,177 Mick Hales; 177 Pat Morrow/First Light; 178 R. Van Nostrand/Photo Researchers; 179 Daniel Heuclin/NHPA; 180,181 Aileen Lotz; 182 George Holton/Photo Researchers; 183 Okapia/Photo Researchers; 184,185 Nevada Wier; 185 (right) Dugald Bremner; 186 Heather Angel; 187 Nevada Wier. ROYAL CHITWAN: 188,189 Galen Rowell; 192 Gerald Cubitt; 194,195 (all) Gerald Cubitt; 196 (left) Gerald Cubitt; 196,197 Len Rue, Jr.; 198 Galen Rowell; 199 Gerald Cubitt; 200,201 Gerald Cubitt; 202 Galen Rowell; 203 (all) Gerald Cubitt; 204 (upper) Leonard Lee Rue III; 204 (lower) Robert & Linda Mitchell; 205 Len Rue, Jr. GUNUNG LEUSER: 206,207 Gerald Cubitt; 210 Gerald Cubitt; 212,213 (all) Gerald Cubitt; 214 (left) Tom McHugh/Photo Researchers; 214,215 Rita Ariyoshi; 216,217 (all) Gerald Cubitt; 218,219 Gerald Cubitt; 220 (all) Gerald Cubitt; 221 (left) Douglas T. Cheeseman, Jr.; 221 (right) Gerald Cubitt; 222 Douglas T. Cheeseman, Jr.; 223 (upper) Gerald Cubitt; 223 (lower) Kjell B. Sandved. ENDPAPERS: George Calef/Masterfile.

All maps that appear in this book are ©Tom Van Sant/The GeoSphere Project

FEATURED PHOTOGRAPHERS

Heather Angel is based in Surrey, England, but spends much of her year abroad, photographing wildlife, plants and landscapes. Her latest book highlights the diversity of London's Kew Gardens.

George Calef is currently a game warden at Chobe National Park in Botswana. He has photographed wildlife at some of the world's most intriguing national parks.

Gerald Cubitt is based in Cape Town, South Africa, and specializes in photographing the wildlife and wilderness of Africa, Asia and, most recently, New Zealand. His past books include *Wild India*, *Wild Malaysia*, and *Wild Indonesia*.

Jay Dickman currently resides in Colorado, and specializes in outdoor location photography. He is the recipient of many awards, including the top prize in the World Press Photo competition, and the 1983 Pulitzer Prize for his coverage of the war in El Salvador.

Gerry Ellis is based in Portland, Oregon, and specializes in photographing endangered species and habitats. He lectures throughout North America and England on the environment, and is at work on a series of three books.

Wolfgang Kaehler lives in Seattle, Washington, but spends most of the year away from home. He has photographed in over 120 countries, and also lectures for photography organizations and museums.

Frans Lanting, a resident of California, is one of the world's leading magazine assignment photographers. He has earned many honors, and was named 1991 BBC Wildlife Photographer of the Year.

Tim Liversedge is a professional filmmaker and winner of numerous awards. He is one of the leading authorities on the Pel's fishing owl and the Okavango Delta. He lives in Maun, Botswana.

Jeff Rotman, 1991 BBC Wildlife Photographer of the Year (Underwater), is based in Somerville, Massachusetts, and has devoted the last year to photographing sharks.

ACKNOWLEDGMENTS

The editors wish to thank the following persons:
Elizabeth Cameron, Rory Gilsenan, Irene Huang, Daniel McBain, Geneviève Monette, Odette Sévigny, Maggie Siggins, Gareth L. Steen.